TRAGIC MAGIC

TRAGIC MAGIC

The Life and Crimes of a Heroin Addict

STUART L. HILLS
St. Lawrence University

RON SANTIAGO

NELSON-HALL PUBLISHERS
Chicago

Project Editor: Rachel Schick
Cover Designer: Sandi Lawrence

Library of Congress Cataloging-in-Publication Data

Hills, Stuart L.
    Tragic magic : the life and crimes of a heroin addict / Stuart L. Hills
and Ron Santiago.
        p.   cm.
    ISBN 0-8304-1354-5.–ISBN 0-8304-1317-0 (pbk.)
    1. Hills, Stuart L.   2. Narcotic addicts—New York (N.Y.)—
Biography.   3. Heroin habit—New York (N.Y.)   4. Narcotics and
crime—New York (N.Y.)   I. Santiago, Ron.   II. Title.
HV5805.S26A3   1992
362.29'3'092—dc20
    [B]   91-35768
                                                                  CIP

Manufactured in the United States of America

10   9   8   7   6   5   4   3   2

TM   The paper used in this book meets the
minimum requirements of American
National Standard for Information
Sciences—Permanence of Paper for
Printed Library Materials, ANSI
Z39.48-1984.

CONTENTS

v

ACKNOWLEDGMENTS

I'M DEEPLY GRATEFUL TO MARY Haught, Laurie Olmstead, and Bonnie Enslow for their careful preparation of the transcripts of the taped interviews with Ron Santiago and the typing of the edited manuscript. Wilma Hills read the entire manuscript in its later stages. Her editorial suggestions and enthusiastic support and encouragement for this project were invaluable. Nelson-Hall editor Rachel Schick skillfully guided the book through the final editorial and production process. I am also grateful to St. Lawrence University for a Piskor Professor Research Grant that facilitated the completion of this project.

Without the trust, good humor, candor, and perseverance of Ron Santiago, *Tragic Magic* would never have been completed. I hope he finds the end result faithful to the spirit and authenticity of his life.

—SLH

INTRODUCTION

Ron Santiago had been out of
the halfway house for only a couple of months when I first
met him. A colleague of mine had invited Ron to talk to his
counseling class about some of Ron's experiences with drugs
and suggested that as a sociologist, I ought to get acquainted
with this intriguing person. I arranged a meeting with Ron,
a forty-two-year-old black man of Cuban ancestry who is a
recovering heroin addict. He told me a little of himself, his
recent experiences in drug treatment programs, and a bit
about his criminal past.

At the time, Ron was barely surviving on welfare, trying
to stay clean from drugs, and attempting to put his life
together in a small town in northern New York, far from the
streets of Harlem and the South Bronx. When I invited him
to talk to my criminology class, he seemed eager to and
interested in sharing his experiences with a college audience.
The students in my class were mesmerized as they listened
to the accounts of this articulate man who had been deeply
engulfed in the life of a dope addict; a man who had committed hundreds of robberies and burglaries to finance his
drug habit; who had worked as a numbers runner and oper-
ated his own drug selling network; who had frequently
manipulated and slipped through the flawed and sometimes

corrupt criminal justice system; who knew personally of men thrown off third floor tiers of brutal jails like New York City's Rikers Island; who had been deeply thrust into the violence, the illicit contraband, the corruption of correctional officers; who understood the dynamics of inmate subcultures in several New York State prisons—and, yet, a man who was attempting to turn his life around.

Perhaps most jarring for these mostly white, affluent college students was the authenticity and humanity of the man who appeared before them: a father who loved and missed his teenage daughter; an accomplished musician who wrote poetry; a man who volunteered his time as facilitator in a Narcotics Anonymous program in a nearby state prison; a strikingly handsome man with charm and wit who had committed serious crimes that had victimized scores of innocent people, yet who did not deny or excuse his behavior, but rather showed remorse now for many of his crimes. As a self-avowed "dope fiend," Ron punctured many of the one-dimensional, media-reinforced stereotypes that so many students and other Americans have of the street-level black and Hispanic heroin addict.

When I suggested to Ron that his fascinating life might be worth sharing with other audiences in the form of a book, he embraced the idea with both enthusiasm and trepidation. From May, 1990 through February, 1991, we spent countless hours tape-recording his story in a series of loosely structured sessions, each of which lasted from two to three hours, during which I asked him about different aspects of his life. *Tragic Magic* (a street term for heroin) is the result, an edited and condensed narrative of Ron Santiago's life story as told to me and presented in his own colorful style. His story, of course, is revealed through the prism of a recovering drug addict looking back at the destructive, though at times alluring, aspects of the world of a street heroin addict and dealer. Undoubtedly, the story would appear somewhat different if I had met Ron years earlier on the street hustling as a frantic junkie—sticking up fast food joints and dodging the police and overdoses—well before this current stage in his recovery process that is still tenuous, uncertain, and unfolding. It is likely that his rendering of some aspects of his experiences as a criminal addict, along with his attempt to make some sense out of his life, bear the coloration of the perspectives gleaned from his rehabilitative experiences in various treatment programs. Also, his responses may have been partly influenced by the way I framed my own probing questions as a sociologist and criminologist, although I tried to refrain from offering my own analysis or moral judgments as he related his experiences to me.

Ron's story is told in his own words and from his own perspective. Except for editing for clarity and readability, and the alteration of most names to conceal personal identities, I have left the account the way he presented it. Although there are many sociological and social policy issues raised by the events revealed in this story, I decided to resist the temptation to add my own interpretative analysis. By looking at the life of one man, *Tragic Magic*, I hope, makes its own distinct contribution to our understanding of the dynamics of drug addiction and the special problems that entrapment in the life of a heroin addict creates for the urban ghetto dweller.

—SLH

1

TRAGIC MAGIC

ONCE I INJECTED HEROIN INTO my system, the whole world changed both physically and mentally. My perception of things changed. The first thing that happened to me was that I just didn't give a fuck about anything. I mean I could have been in a basement during an earthquake, and the building could have shaken and everything could have fallen right down on top of me at that time, but it would have been all right because I was high. You know, it's sort of like you're pulling the connected plugs on the outside world. I was self-contained. I didn't want anything else, except more dope. I didn't want anybody to invade my space. Physically, it was a warm feeling. You get a warm glow in the crack of your ass, and then the warmth spreads throughout your body and your body starts to slow down. Even though I injected drugs, I could still get the quinine taste in my throat. And then my head would start to slow down. It was like my world would start to go in slow motion.

When I first got involved in heroin it was a pretty potent drug. In the beginning I would spend maybe the first forty-five minutes to an hour, maybe two hours, just nodding. I didn't want to get up. I didn't want to take a piss, I didn't want to eat, I didn't want to wash, I didn't want to do anything. So before I got high, I would make sure I was in a place or

1

situation where I didn't have to go anywhere or do anything. I would either be at my house, a friend's house, or some place where I didn't have to physically move for a long time.

There's a physical addiction that goes along with the psychological, which makes heroin such tragic magic, as they sometimes call it. The physical addiction is that your body, in withdrawal, begins to ache. I mean physically ache—your muscles, your joints. Your stomach cramps up. Like there's no food in it, but the cramps are very painful. It's like somebody sticks a giant needle in your spine and sucks out all the fluid out of your bones and all you're left with is raw nerves. You can't sit down. You're very agitated. You're very aggravated. Even your bowels change in withdrawal. You get the runs and everything. When you're shooting heroin, however, you're constipated, and don't even take a shit. It slows down all of your body processes. All of them. And in order for your body to function, you have to maintain a certain level of the drug in your system. When this level starts to drop, you start to feel withdrawal symptoms. You start to feel pain.

Every once in a while in the beginning you try to play this game, this psychological game with dope, about how you don't really need it. So I guess your mind is trying to tell your body, don't get sick. Or you're feeling the symptoms, but mentally you're telling yourself you're not feeling them or you won't give in. You'll deal with the pain even though it's a light pain at first. You'll deal with it until you can't deal with it anymore. There were times when physically I had to get high almost every two hours, because otherwise I would get violently ill to the point where my hands were shaking. You know, I was starting to fall apart. My muscles weren't really coordinated and I would start to convulse. And the longer you're abstinent, away from the drug, the worse these symptoms become. But again, there were times that I'd have to play mind games, because I didn't have the money for the dope, and I was out in the street and I had to hustle or scramble to do something. I knew it was going to take me three or four hours, and I just had to deal with the pain of the withdrawal symptoms. So there were many times when I woke up in the morning or even during the day and I was sick as a dog but I had to go out.

Only in the beginning and a very few other times during my life did I really get high—experience that fantastic euphoric feeling. Looking back at it now, every shot after the first shot that I ever took of heroin, I tried to get the same effect I got the first time. That dream kept me strung out for years, trying to get back to that point. But you lose something in the process, because you go straight from being sick to just being okay or nodding out off of the drug. There is no in-between level anymore, and this is what I tried to find. I always tried to find that level where I could float. Yet there were very few times where I could manage to get that feeling. When I had money I would just come home and I would shoot the dope. First it would take the sickness off and then I would wait for that good feeling to come down on me, but it seems like I would take the express elevator. I would either start nodding, or I would just be feeling okay. Not good enough for everything around me to blend in like it used to when I first started getting high. I no longer could experience that feeling of serenity and well-being. There was no feeling of being at peace with the world; no longer that special dreamy sensation of floating and total relaxation. It seems like after a while that middle point just leaves you. And there are very, very few times where I was high and enjoyed it after the first few years of shooting heroin.

MY DAY WOULD ACTUALLY START the night before. Most of the time I would be thinking, "Where am I going to get my wake-up shot?" Every dope fiend I know is concerned about his wake-up shot. You've got to have a shot of dope in the morning. As soon as you wake up, the first thing you want to do is get high so you can start your day. Starting your day sick is not preferable. It's not something that you want to do. If I didn't have something going for me the night before or something immediately in the morning, I would wake up terrified because I wouldn't know what I had to do that day to get some money. There were many mornings I woke up and didn't know where I was going to get my first shot of dope, or when I was going to get it, or what I had to do to get money to get that shot of dope.

I couldn't save dope. If dope was around, I would shoot it. While I was getting high off that last bit of dope, I was justifying it in my head that I'll be okay in the morning or something will come through, but I really saved my worry until the morning. And I used to do this all the time. As soon as I got high, I would worry about tomorrow, tomorrow. But in actuality, I started worrying about tomorrow as that shot started to wear off. I'd become more and more terrified. God damn it, I'm going to wake up without my dope. What am I going to do? The reason you want to get that wake-up shot is to give you that edge, so that whatever you have to do in the morning, whether you're boosting, you're stealing or whatever, at least you're going to have some dope in your system to steady your nerves. Because if you're going on a burglary or going on a "guis" [a job or heist] and you're sick, you tend to make mistakes, do something that you don't want to do or something that you shouldn't do, or something you can't do. You've got to be straight, because you're weak, too, when you're sick. Being straight means having enough dope in you to steady your nerves, to take the edge off your sickness, but not enough heroin in your system to get high. If you're going on a burglary and you're so goddamn weak you can't open a window, you aren't going to get in. If you're going to stick somebody up and you're standing there shaking and everything, you're not going to intimidate people. So you've got to have some dope to steady you. Not so much for mental courage, as much as physical coordination. There were times when I had to drive somewhere and I couldn't drive I was so goddamn sick. So when I wake up in the morning and I don't have any dope and I don't have any way of getting any, I usually try to get somebody to turn me on in the morning. Promise him anything. You know, like, "Stuart, if you turn me on right now—I've got this burglary over here—but I've got to be straight first." Sometimes it works.

In the morning there were dope spots—places where you bought dope. As an active dope fiend, you would go hang around some of these guys in the morning. You would even ask one of the pushers to give you some dope. Depending upon the relationship you had, he might give you one or two bags just to take the edge off. You get that sickness down a little bit so you can go do what you want to do. But then you'd have to come back later on and take care of the bill.

There isn't too much credit in the dope world. We don't really have very good credit backgrounds. And we've been known to promise them anything. But that's part of the dope fiend life.

So I would go around to one of the dope spots, because this is where everybody comes to buy their dope anyway. It's sort of like a meeting place, because you meet everybody who's ready to go out in the morning and do whatever they have to do. It's like a union hall, or something like that, where guys come in and see what's available today. There were some days where I would go around to the spots and the pusher wouldn't give me any dope and I couldn't con anybody else out of turning me on to some dope. But somebody would come along and need somebody either as a lookout or a participant or something. Or somebody is willing to take you along on what they're getting ready to do. Of course, you'd end up doing the dirty part of whatever it is that they had to do. I mean, it's going to be dirty anyway, but you end up doing the dirtiest part of the dirty job because you're the one that needs the dope. But you don't balk at that too much, because you had to get that dope; so if this is what you have to do, you do it. Most of the time I did run into somebody who was ready to do something, or somebody who scored the night before or early in the morning. Sometimes I would leave my house and be in the street by 7:30 or 8:00 in the morning, because you've got guys strung out who have legit jobs and they've got to get their shot of dope. So before they go to work, they come down, they cop, they get high, and they go to work. They'd be to work by 9:00, they'd be high, but they'd be on the job. There are so many people coming by these spots that you run into somebody who's either going to turn you on or get you involved with whatever they're getting ready to do. And this is where I became like a jack-of-all-trades. I didn't give a shit. I didn't care what you were doing. Robbing a bank, sticking up the President, snatching kids—I didn't care what you did. If I could become part of that and get some money, I was game.

So you see, a dope fiend's life or day runs in cycles. You've got morning, mid-morning, afternoon, evening, and then late night. You've got night people, day people, afternoon people.

The dope was everywhere—neighborhoods, parks. I mean, you could walk in the street and pick out the dope fiends there and know what they're doing at what particular time. Who just got high, how they got high. It's a whole subculture. And you learn to identify and participate in that subculture. I could buy dope anywhere. I could walk on any street in New York City, and they would know I was a dope fiend, which made it easy to buy dope from anybody, even though they don't sell dope to everybody. You know, people could be cops, and people might be setting you up.

As soon as I had cash in my hand, wherever I was at, I would go buy some dope right away. In the early days, most of the time I carried my works (needle, eye dropper, and bottle cap) with me. If I went on a burglary and all we got were TVs, obviously, you couldn't do anything with that, so we would have to go to a fence and sell the TV. I wanted my money and I wanted my money quick; and as soon as I got my money I wanted to turn around and buy some dope, so that meant I had to have my works, too. And this is really stupid, because when you go on these burglaries or on these jobs and you get busted, possession of works is another charge, but you really don't give a shit about that, because you don't think about being busted. Nine times out of ten you don't get busted anyway, but you want your works right with you and you don't want to wait. So if I'm in Queens, I don't want to wait to come all the way back to the Bronx to buy some dope. If I'm in Queens and I get money for whatever I got in Queens, I want to buy some dope right then and there—then I'll come back to the Bronx. If I'm sick, man, I need dope right now. Sometimes the sickness is bad, though, and you end up getting involved in a situation or getting busted doing it because you can't wait.

THERE WERE TIMES IN MY LIFE when I was tired—physically, emotionally and psychologically tired of living this way. But I had forged such a lifestyle that I didn't know how to live any other way. I mean, you could take me away from the South Bronx. You could take me away from Harlem. You could transplant me to any other place in the world and I wouldn't know how to live unless I was shooting dope and living in the drug subculture. You get used to the lifestyle despite the things you have to do to get that money to buy that dope. This becomes your routine. Like a person who gets up and goes to work every day has their ritual that they go through: they get up, they wash, they have coffee, breakfast, they get dressed, they take a train or drive to work, and they interrelate with the people on the job. This becomes like second nature, a routine for them that they get used to. When these people take vacations they're kind of lost, because they're used to working in a certain routine, a certain schedule every day. The dope world is the same way. You don't just use the drug and then continue on a different type of life; you live a drug life. Everything you do revolves around getting money to buy dope to get high. Your entire lifestyle changes, because the main focal point in your life is getting money to buy dope to get high. Everything else is secondary.

You definitely get strung out on playing with the needle, because that's part of the pull—part of the attraction. That's how you get the dope in your system. So there is a ritual around the needle and the bottle cap that you use to mix your dope with water; you heat it and then draw it up. I mean, what you're saying is like, I've got this fucking dope now. So I would take my time and try to stretch it out. But it's part of a ritual, because you know that by the time you get to your works that you've already got the dope and that the feeling that you've looking for is only seconds away. I used to be strung out on water shots, because I could get my works working and it would be satisfying psychologically. I would put water in the cooker and possibly get some residue from the hundreds of other shots. I was strung out on fixing the works, getting the water in there, cooking up the water and just injecting the shit on my own. This was part of my ritual. This was part of my life. The works are the vital point, because by the time you get to the works you've got the dope. Every time that you relate to those works, the dope is there. So it's a very crucial point. I mean, you can't even think about using the works if you have no dope. And the works are what you use to inject—that's your connection. You connect the dope to your body through the works.

I've had quite a few of my friends overdose. I remember

one kid in particular when I was in the Job Corps. We were living in Massachusetts, and we had come down to New York City for Thanksgiving. We had been relatively drug-free up in the Job Corps; I mean we had drugs, but not as much or as often as we would have wanted. His nickname was Squid. And we had come home to the Bronx and I was trying to persuade Squid to go with me to get high and then he could go home. But he was with Jamie and he decided to go to his house. I said, "All right, I'll give you a call after I go get straight and you go get straight and we'll hang out; we'll go downtown to dance." I bought some dope, I went home, and I forgot all about calling Squid that night. I called him Saturday, the next morning, and nobody answered the phone. We were down in the city for like six days, I think. The day before we were supposed to go back, I still couldn't get in touch with him, so I went over to his neighborhood. That's when I found out from his sister he died that first night we came down. He had bought some dope and he had OD'd. His death didn't stop me from getting high, but emotionally it touched me. I guess because he was really, really that close; he was the first casualty that close to me.

I tried to be cautious and careful after that but when it comes to dope you throw your caution and care out the window. I mean, injecting yourself with heroin during those days, you almost had to be like a doctor. You had to wrap a piece of matchbook cover around the bottom tip of the eyedropper to make the connection tight between it and the needle. And then you had to inject yourself and regulate the shot as it was going in. There was a thing we called booting after you got a hit. A hit is when you get the needle in the vein and booting is allowing the blood to come up and mix with the dope in the eyedropper and pushing this mixture back in the vein several times. Some guys go boot crazy because they like to see the blood come up and down; they're called boot freaks. But if you get so much as an air bubble in your veins, you die. I'm surprised a lot of people lasted all these years.

Dope fiends will even try to find the dope that caused another addict to overdose, because you want the best you can get for your money. And you'll live with this fantasy that you'll just inject a little bit, not enough to go out, which means that you could stretch that dope more. But most dope fiends that I know are greedy, too. They would gladly risk overdosing trying to get higher. I did it myself. Sometimes we would hear—we would get the word—that, "Yo man, that dope in Brooklyn is some killer dope." So we would go around there looking for it; we would have a vague idea where it was. We would go around to the neighborhood, usually to a park, a corner, a bar, and we would ask people, "Who has the dope?" We heard the neighborhood and the name, and half the time that's all we had.

I remember one time we went to a park in Brooklyn and there was a lot of dealers there; and as soon as you walk in you have to check things out first, you know, see what's what. And I remember this guy—I saw him by a garbage can and he was bent over. I thought he was dead. I looked down and he was just real out of it, but when I kicked him, he moved. I looked and I saw his arms; he had tracks on them. Chico wanted to go to some dealer that he saw on the other side of the park who he had gotten word was the guy with the good dope. I said, "Hold up, man, wait a minute, wait a minute." I bent down and asked this guy where he bought the dope from and I eventually got out of him something like "blue tape." I don't know, he was delirious. So that's what we went and bought, man, some blue tape, good dope.

A SHOOTING GALLERY IS A PLACE where addicts gather to shoot drugs. A lot of times you can't just buy dope and go home and shoot drugs. Buying drugs was one problem; shooting them ended up being another problem, because you never wanted to take that home, and you couldn't do it out in public because people would see you. So every neighborhood has what's called a shooting gallery, which is essentially an empty apartment, another addict's apartment or someone else's place, and he allows addicts to come in and shoot drugs in his apartment for a fee that is anywhere from two to five dollars. Some shooting galleries you have to bring your own works, and the only thing that you have there is the space that's provided for you to use your drugs. In other places, the guy who's running the shooting gallery will rent you a set of works for a price, again two to five dollars. Most of these places are dirty, filthy—nobody really bothers to clean them because nobody really cares; all they care about is a space where they can shoot their drugs. Addicts are not the only ones who know about these shooting galleries. The police know about them also, and frequently they raid the places because they know that at any given time they're liable to find anywhere from ten to twenty addicts that are shooting drugs. Many of these shooting galleries are protected; they have guys at the door who only let in known addicts. If you're not known the guy will ask to see your tracks before he lets you in. If you don't have any tracks in your arms, you're not getting in.

In the sixties we shared needles. The guy who ran the house usually would clean the works after every person got off. Sometimes he would use bleach or he'd boil the needles in water and clean the little eye droppers out with Q-tips as best he could. In the late seventies and eighties with the AIDS thing coming out and with the switch from eye droppers to syringes, needles got more disposable because they were readily available. We were stealing them out of hospitals like crazy. The works were in brand new packages. You'd get a sealed package with a syringe in it. As soon as you walk in you pay for your works and get off.

If I had just gotten some money, bought some dope and was across town, most of the time I would try to get to a shooting gallery because it would be a safer place than just going into an alley or up onto a roof somewhere. In the early sixties it was okay. People would walk by and see you shooting up and they'd just go on about their business or they'd turn around and leave because they would be scared. But in the seventies and eighties, with this anti-drug thing started, they would either say something to you—they would yell at you—or call the police. The average rooftop in a tenement district or in a high-dope district was littered with dope bags, used needles, everything. All types of paraphernalia. In the late seventies and eighties, neighborhoods were starting to come out against it, because outside of shooting galleries, rooftops and hallways were the best places that we used to go since basically all you needed was your works. I know some guys who used to carry around a little bottle of water. So you'd have your water, you'd have your cooker, you'd have your works. All you'd need was a bag of dope. And some guys do get that desperate where they'll get off anywhere. I mean, I've gotten off on a subway, bus, taxicab, while walking down the street, rooftop; go to somebody's house and get off in their bathroom; walk in your house—"Hi, Stuart, can I use your bathroom for a minute?"

By the 1980s, AIDS was a real concern, so most people tried to make sure that they had their own set of works. Before, I would lend you my set of works, and you would lend it to other guys—five of us might be together. All we would need was one set of works, because one guy would use it and then the next guy in line would clean it out with water. They would clean out the blood and squirt water through the needle itself; clean the blood out of the needle to your satisfaction and then you fix up your dope. Then when you finish you give it to the next man, he cleans it out, and so on. That stopped in the eighties because of AIDS. So even in the shooting galleries, every time you got high, you wanted to use a different set of works. But hey, when you want to get high, and there's only one set of works there and you know that these works are AIDS-infected, you'll rinse that shit out and use them. That's part of the denial of the disease too, because just like when you get involved shooting heroin in the beginning, you don't think that you're going to get strung out. You're going to be the only one in ten million people who uses this drug, and doesn't get strung out. Just like with AIDS—you're going to get high, but you're not going to get AIDS. Even if you were to go to the hospital and have them give you a blood test and they say, "Yo man, you got AIDS," you aren't going to believe that. Sometimes you're in such a goddamn rush that you don't clean the blood out. You "skeet" it through—you run the works through water once or twice, and you start to fix your own shot, man, you want to get high.

THIS MIGHT SOUND STRANGE, but I didn't really have any feelings at all toward the people I stole from. I mean, it was business, nothing personal. It was business. I never really knew most of my victims—the ones that I stuck up anyway. There were people that I knew, that I wanted to stick up, and I did. I didn't give a fuck what they thought; I still don't. But the burglaries and other robberies were just a bunch of numbers and faces. I never really got close to my victims, so I never really got to know them. The drive was to get the money for the dope. I couldn't let anything interfere with that. I never really felt squeamish about some of that shit that I did. After I got high, I would sort of feel bad a little. But the thought would only be there for a little while and then the dope would wash it away. The first time I went into rehab, I felt shitty about a lot of stuff I did. But at the immediate time that I did it, honestly, I didn't give a fuck, you know, I didn't care. I had to have that money for dope. And if they came in between that, man, they came in between that. Nothing personal, strictly business. At one point I even stole from my mother and grandmother. I felt bad about it, but obviously not bad enough to stop doing it. But if the opportunity was there, I did it. And I would come back into the house the next day and they would know, and I would feel bad for a little while, but if I got sick again and I needed money, that's the first thought that came in my mind—if it was there, I did it.

2

CHAPTER

GROWING UP IN THE GHETTO

I FIRST STARTED USING DRUGS when I was living in Manhattan. I was about twelve or thirteen years old, and it was more or less a peer type thing, because for the fellas it was something illegal, something bad to do. All the people we knew in Harlem were either drinking or using heavy drugs. At this point in my life, I couldn't see the correlation between heavy drugs and what it really did to you, because most of the people I saw who were drug addicts or alcoholics were bums. But I used to see a lot of people like the hustlers and the numbers runners. These guys were also involved in drugs, but I saw a big difference between them, with all their flash and money, and the guy lying in the sidewalk.

I first tried alcohol when I was around twelve years old. I had some gin and some rum. A bunch of us guys who used to go to elementary school together got a bottle that a friend had gotten from his house and we drank it. From the first taste I knew I never would like alcohol—it burned, I didn't like the way it tasted, I hated the way it smelled, and I hated the way I felt. I really never got into drinking a lot. When we moved to the Bronx, I went to junior high school there, and I got into a different crowd; it was a different variety of friends than the people I knew in Harlem. Living in

13

Harlem was like a closed society. It was mainly blacks, and I just got used to living in a small community. When I got to the Bronx it was a much looser community. There were people coming in from different parts of the city and it was just a bigger community. There was always one of the guys in the group that I was hanging out with that was experimenting with something; and they would come back and let us know how this is, how that is, how this affects them, how you felt after that.

At one point we were at a party and pot was being passed around, so at this time I smoked some reefer. The pot made me laugh a lot. In the surroundings I was in, I was comfortable with everybody and I was having a good time. I had the reefer with some wine. There was a couple of females there, some good music, and it was me and a couple of guys and it was a real pleasant setting. I had never done it before so I was asking everybody how I'm supposed to feel. And I'm observing other people who are just laughing, so I smoked it and I started to feel high, to feel loose. But I noticed that it was a different head than the wine I was drinking; it was like I was high off the two things at the same time. And I sort of liked the pot at that time, not really enough to constantly go ahead and use it, but I knew the effect. It was a while after that before I tried pot again.

When I moved to the Bronx I really got into Latin music and that was when I started getting into my Latin roots; and part of that was going to a lot of Latin dances. In New York at the time, Latin dances were all over the city and I remember a particular dance in Brooklyn. I was with three other Latin guys who had money, so we bought some rum, which they drank. At that point I didn't want to deal with the alcohol, but we bought a nickel bag of reefer and we got like twenty-one joints out of the bag. So by the time we got to the dance I was feeling pretty good. And that's when I started to notice it wasn't a giggly, laughing type of head; it was sort of a mental high. I felt at the time that it enhanced my sense of hearing, seeing. I was getting in tune with things that normally if I wasn't high, I wouldn't be aware of. But because I was high off pot, I could stare at things and I would see things in my mind. I guess you could call it mild hallucinations, because I later went on to try acid and there's a big difference between acid and pot. But I felt pretty good; I felt like I was in control. It was a good feeling.

At this time drugs weren't really that expensive. I would ask my mother for money and she would give me money. And I would just buy drugs with it as opposed to what I told her I wanted the money for. I would ask her for ten dollars and she would give me twenty dollars. So I had extra money to buy it. A bag of pot with twenty-one joints in it would last me about a week, unless I got together with the fellas and shared pot. At this point marijuana just didn't cost that much, plus everybody always had some. To buy a bag of pot, five guys could get together and each chip in one dollar. But I wouldn't even characterize my use as being on a regular basis, because when I got into other drugs I just left pot alone. In fact, my getting high was a weekend thing. Monday through Friday was school time or different things, and at this point in my life I just didn't think about getting high every day.

In the beginning, drugs were a recreational weekend activity, but there came a time when it definitely progressed. When I was younger, I spent a lot of time with the guys that were just using pot and alcohol. Because I didn't like the alcohol, I would fake it more or less. I would drink the alcohol because everybody else did but I sort of liked the pot when we did get high. But I couldn't see what the other drugs were like. Heroin was a concept that I couldn't conceive of. I thought that all heroin addicts and people that heavily drink alcohol eventually turned up in the gutters and streets, and I didn't want to do that so I figured the best way was not to use heroin and not to drink. And I wish I could have kept that fear. Later, because of running around with different people, I got into different types of drugs. I even had my hippie years where I did a lot of pills, a lot of acid, and a lot of speed. I was about seventeen, eighteen years old when I started experimenting heavily with pills: Seconal, Tylenol, Valium, Librium, Reds, Black Beauties—a whole bunch of other pills I can't even remember. My hippie crowd had them all the time. Pills are one of the things I just never spent money on because most of the people that I knew that were in it always had pills and they gave them to me.

I used to listen to this soul music, so I would go to the Apollo all the time and that type of crowd was mainly a drinking crowd. When I moved up to the Bronx and my musical horizons started to expand, I got into Jimi Hendrix and the hard rock, which later got termed acid rock. This type of music was generally associated with the hippie crowd. They got into mind-expanding psychedelic drugs, because they thought that the pills would take them places, whereas the alcohol and the pot just couldn't get them there. There was a lot of pot going around because among those particular drugs pot was the mildest of them all. But after the pills started to take effect they can take you in a different direction. I was scared to death of acid for two or three years before I even decided to take some, and I took only some mild acid. But by that time I had already been shooting crystal meth, pure speed. I also used to sniff methedrine, amphetamines. My body used to just constantly go; there were times I couldn't sleep, maybe four or five days at a time. But again, these are the people that used to hang out in the Village, go to Fillmore East, hang out with the hard rock groups, and their lifestyle was different. So I could leave the Bronx and go downtown and hang out with them and I would be into the pills. Then I would come back up to the Bronx and would get back into the booze and the reefer.

I eventually got tired of that because it just wasn't doing for me what I wanted when I looked for an escape, which is really what it was. During this time I started to get a real habit because I liked to stay up. And you really speed when you go up—like when you start getting high—but then you crash and crash heavy. And that was one of the things that really prompted me to get into heroin, because I wanted to get into a down. I liked the up but I didn't like the crash. I didn't like the feeling when you were coming off the drug, and if you go up you want to take something to smooth your way coming down.

I would say around 1963 a heavy transition started. You could see it all over the city: heroin had come to stay. And everybody was doing it. At first it was recreational, but being young I really couldn't see the long-term effects of heroin. The one or two people who were pointed out to me as hardcore junkies were so far alienated from my lifestyle or from where I was at that time—I couldn't see any way in the world that I would eventually end up like that.

THE FIRST TIME I USED HEROIN I was with a buddy of mine, Chico, and Lenny and Jamie, guys from the St. Mary's projects in the Bronx on Jackson Avenue. I was about twelve or thirteen years old and most of my friends were about the same age. This was my group: we played basketball together, went to school together, joined gangs together. We used to get our haircuts together, we used to hang out at everybody's house—we did everything together. Chico was always the leader, and I eventually developed an attachment with him and his family because I didn't have a family. I lived alone with my mother. I never knew my father and I was an only child. Chico didn't have a big brother, and he and I were more or less the same age so we started hanging out. But Chico was always a little more streetwise than most of us.

One Friday in the summertime, Chico, Lenny, and Jamie had some pot and we were on our way to the liquor store. When we got to the liquor store, Chico said, "I got some dope and I'm going to get high. If you want to all get high you got to chip in." So we kicked up a couple of dollars. We had the dope, we had the booze, and we had the reefer and we all went to Jamie's house. They told me at first that they didn't want me to get involved, but I had this macho thing—the hell with that, if they want to get high, I want to get high. I had been experimenting with some of these other drugs and I ain't dead yet, so I wanted to check it out. They didn't let me shoot it this time—I sniffed the dope. I think back now and I think psychologically I didn't get the effect I wanted because I wanted to shoot the dope like the rest of them.

I felt the quinine going down my throat, and I sort of pushed it to the back of my mind, because by this time I had already learned that in order to get the drugs into your system some of them had a nasty taste. In order to reach the head you wanted, especially with pills and stuff, there was like a waiting period. Even with the pills, I would pop one or two and then I would drink some beer or something behind it and wait or do something for maybe forty-five minutes, depending on how long it took the pills to get the desired effect. With the heroin it was almost *instantaneous* when I sniffed it. I got a warm feeling all over my body and my body got high, sort of like morphine; you know, morphine doesn't really get your head high, it gets your whole body high. It wasn't like a psychedelic drug—it's the complete opposite—but I started to feel real relaxed, real, real relaxed and real slow, real slow.

I didn't like the fact that the quinine burned going down my nose but the effect it had was a real warm and pleasant sensation, and I started to drift, dream. No problems, I mean, I'm like watching everybody else and it seems like the world is starting to go around in slow motion and I was sort of out there in space just drifting as we walked in the street—it was just a different sensation, a different feeling.

Everything was different and the high lasted for quite a few hours, but again, I didn't like the burning sensation going down my nose. So the next day we went back up to Jamie's house and I had what is called skin-pop. They cooked it up in a wine bottle cap. I would buy a bottle of wine, drink a little bit, and give the rest of the wine away because all I wanted was the bottle cap. We used glass eyedroppers and needles that we would steal from hospitals—just walk into the hospitals, find out where they were at, wait for your chance and take the needles. Or we would buy them from someone who worked in the hospital or someone in the street who had needles. We'd use one needle, run some water through it and all of us would use that one needle. At the time the biggest fear was what we called blood poisoning: if you didn't rinse the needle out good enough and you injected somebody else's blood, you would just get like the chills. I was scared of needles. But I made myself forget about that fear, mainly because I couldn't show fear with the fellas. I had to be just as much a man as they were. And at that point it was just a matter of injecting it into the fat part of my arm and I watched the other guys go through it. I was still fearful but when my turn came I didn't show it.

I liked heroin. I liked it. By that time, I had experimented with every drug that I had wanted to experiment with. Every drug that they had out on the market—pill form, powder form, liquid form—I had experimented with them all. I just couldn't find a head I liked, a recreational drug that I felt comfortable with, but when I got to heroin all that changed. That first time I injected dope I got a *fantastic* high. The first time. And looking back, every other time after that is trying to feel like that first high. I spent over twenty years trying to do that. It just doesn't happen.

After I was already involved six or seven months, people started telling me about the bad side. In the beginning I had used heroin recreationally, like on weekends, but during the days in between shots I started to feel jumpy or jittery or something. I started to change and I really didn't know why. I figured I would just start getting high on the weekends, and leave it alone from Sunday night until the next Friday or Saturday. But physically my body started to change; mentally I started to change, too. I was agitated a lot and I didn't know why. After three or four days I started to feel comfortable again but then it was time to start getting high again. I started to notice that when I got high I didn't feel agitated any more, I didn't feel on edge, I didn't feel nervous or jumpy, easily excitable. Mentally I didn't know that the craving I had was for the drugs. Because at that point I still was concentrating on school but I knew something was different. I couldn't concentrate on my studies like I wanted to.

I was in seventh grade, junior high school, at the time. And I really didn't know what it was and then it just got where I started to look forward to getting high on the weekends. But again, all this is in retrospect, because at the time I couldn't see that I was gradually getting sucked into the physical and psychological dependence on heroin. Things just didn't seem right until I got high, and when I got high everything was okay. It made going through that week all right. I went along like this using heroin just on weekends for about two months. And then I had a big change—I got high on a Tuesday. I remember that day, because the last time I got high was a Sunday. I can't remember who suggested to me that I was strung out and that in order to make everything okay I had to get high not just on the weekends, but I know it was suggested to me on a Tuesday.

In the beginning some of the older guys in the gang tried

to discourage us from using heroin, but we just never listened, because we were feeling too good. We'd say, "I'm not getting strung out, something else is wrong, and who are you to tell me to stop? Why don't you stop? You're telling me to stop, but you're asking me for money so you can go buy dope to get high." The bigger guys even used to kick our ass sometimes when they used to see us in the neighborhood getting ready to buy dope. They knew what we were doing and they'd come over there and they'd kick our ass, and they'd chase the dope dealer the other way. He was their connection, not ours.

THE NAME OF THE GANG I belonged to was called the Sportsmen. There were two subdivisions and I was in the Sportsmen Tots because I was a little guy. I got into the gang because at that time growing up in New York City was territorial among young people. In whatever four or five block section or group of projects you lived everybody belonged to a gang. I was living at this time in the St. Mary's Projects in the South Bronx. And I belonged to a gang simply because in my neighborhood there was a gang there. In order not to have to go through the hassles of not being a gang member I decided to join the gang.

To belong to the Sportsmen, I had to whip another kid's ass to prove my manhood. I had to drink with them, I had to get high with them to be accepted as one of them. But again, being part of a gang was sort of like alcohol to me. I did it because it was there, but I just never was totally committed to it, because there were some things that the gangs were doing that I was scared of. At this time I was scared of the police and I was scared of jail, because I was hearing stories about what happens to guys in prison. There was a lot of weapons around me, a lot of violence, too. Violence was just something you got used to. There were fights everyday—stabbings, gunfights, everything. But if I didn't belong to a gang, I probably would have been getting my butt kicked every day, getting my money taken all the time, and if I went outside my neighborhood, whether I was in a gang or not, I was prey to whatever gang was in that particular neighborhood.

The guys in my gang were all black with an age range of twelve to thirty-five years old. There were affiliated Sportsmen gangs all over New York, and lots of other gangs such as the Enchanters, the Assassins, the Chaplains, and the Crowns. So if I was to go to another part of the city where there was a Sportsmen or a Sportsmen-affiliated gang, then I could walk in their neighborhood. We used to have sweaters with a coat of arms or emblem, which was kind of dangerous, because if you had to go through another gang's territory to get to your territory and they saw the emblem, you were a target.

We had a reputation of having some bad guys in the gang. They weren't scared of the police or anybody. We always had a lot of guns and we were always ready to fight. It was like hand-to-hand combat, a lot of bricks, sticks, knives. I mean, these were serious rumbles.

Usually a stupid thing would provoke a fight: a comment, a girl liking another guy, a guy wearing the wrong clothes, walking on the wrong side of the street, coming in the wrong neighborhood, or a lot of times it would be another gang member coming in and beating one of our gang members and that would be enough just to get us to go crazy. But in summertime in New York City excuses weren't really needed. There was a lot of gang activity going on.

We had a gang president, a vice president, and a warlord. The warlord was in charge of setting up the battles. If for some reason he felt that we should have a fight with the Chaplains or the Crowns, he'd come back to the block and he'd say, "Yo man, strap up, get your guns, get all your shit, we're going over there." I remember one time going through Forest Projects, the project that was around the school I was going to, but which belonged to a different gang faction. One night Paulie, our warlord, came down and he told Joe and me and the older guys, "We're going to fight the Crowns tonight." One of the Crowns was going with some girl in the Forest Projects who used to go with a Sportsmen, and Paulie had decided that was a violation, which was enough to provoke a war. The warlords got together and they couldn't settle it. So I remember leaving my house in the St. Mary's Projects with other young guys and walking up the block to the Forest Projects. And it reminded me of Attila the Hun because I didn't know we had that many guys in the gang. And by the time we got to the Forest Projects, it was hundreds of guys with guns, rifles, and grenades. The word had been put out that all the Sportsmen gangs were to get together for this particular night.

We shot at the projects, we shot at the cops. Three guys were killed, a lot of guys got bricked and batted and stabbed. I had a rifle and a gun that I got from Juan and Chico. Juan used to have guns all the time. But I didn't shoot anybody that particular night because I was still scared. But for me to go without arms would have meant, you know, that I was a punk. We just whipped them that night. We got everybody and we just walked down Trinity Avenue through the neighborhood. Nobody ran.

There was a time when street gang fighting was nice, when we just did it in the street and people didn't get hurt too bad. But then it started to get real violent and it got to the point where the gangs would come to your house looking for you. People would knock on your door and as soon as you opened the door, they would shoot you or stab you or whatever. Or they would ask your mother or whoever answered the door where you were, and they would either wait for you to come to the door, or they would come through the house looking for you and then hurt you.

One night, Joey, one of the older gang members, was playing cards with some guys and he found out that they were cheating at the game. So he demanded his money back, and since Joey was by himself, they laughed and told him to get the hell out of there—at gun point. So he left. And we were on the stoop when Joey came back into the neighborhood that night. And we said, "Yo Joey, what's up, what's up?" And he didn't say anything to anybody. He just went into his house, grabbed two guns and walked out. We saw what he did, but he still wasn't speaking. He obviously had something on his mind. So we followed him back to where the guys were playing cards, but the card game was over. And he found out where this one guy—I guess who was the cheater at the card game—lived. I forgot the guy's name, but we'll just say John for now. And it turned out the guy lived maybe eight blocks away from where we hung out. So Joey went to John's house and knocked on the door. And John's mother came to the door, and Joey asked, "Where's John?" And John came to the door. So Joey asked him again, "Give me back my money." And the guy says, "Fuck you!" So Joey told him, "Sayonara, motherfucker!" Pow! Shot him twice and walked away.

I stayed active in the Sportsmen gang for about eighteen months and then I got more into other things, especially my new hobby—heroin. And some of the other gang members started to get more into the same thing. Dope started to dilute the power of the gangs because instead of fighting and doing other things, you had to worry about your dope addicts, who weren't very reliable.

When I was with the gang, I wasn't a tough guy. I was with a group of guys so I wasn't really in the forefront, I was in the middle. But when it came time for me to make money for my habit I was out front, and they saw that. With the gangs, I didn't have the reputation as a tough guy or a bad guy. In fact, I was kind of soft because I never really wanted to be up front doing things. I had heart, but I didn't have that much heart. I didn't really want to go to jail so I didn't want to do anything blatant like shoot somebody in a gang fight. I was scared of jail. But if something happened to one of the five or six guys that I was hanging out with then I was like, "All right, to hell with it, let's go down." Anything could happen to any one of the gang members and he could just come around the block and say, "Yo man, let's go down—this dude took my money" or "He took my bike" or he did this or he did that. And because you were a gang member you had to stop what you were doing and go down.

I tore up a lot of property. I threatened a lot of people—I mean, I didn't do the actual threatening but I was there. We'd put a gun to a kid's head and take his money, mostly kids who were members of other gangs. See, we didn't start robbing the grocery stores and other places until the dope came in. At this point, it was just other gang members from other neighborhoods. You know, we would go into other neighborhoods and let them know we were there. Showing face by being with the gang. As a matter of fact, I was careful not to show my face too much when it came to robberies and the other things, because I didn't want to be identified. But I lived in a gang-infested area, so I had to make a choice: join a gang or don't join a gang. It was easier to join.

As I got more into heroin, I kind of drifted away from the gang. Plus, there came a time where a lot of guys were getting busted and going to jail. For a while, the police had a hard time dealing with gang fights. Giving out all those juvenile delinquent cards, you know. The courts were just not built to handle all the cases that they were getting. I was stopped by the police but I was never taken down to juvenile court for any of my gang activity. They would stop me and say, "You're a Sportsmen," or "You're part of this gang" and this and that, but they couldn't prove anything. So they'd hold us for a little while and eventually let us go. Or they'd take our name and threaten us: "Once you get in trouble with the gang you're going to jail!" But since you're around a lot of other gang members you'd say, "You can kiss my ass—I ain't going anywhere."

MY HEROIN HABIT GOT BIGGER than the money I was getting from my mother. Dope used to be two dollars a bag. I used to get high once a day. This is after we forgot about the weekend use; you had to get high everyday. I was about seventeen years old and on my way to dropping out of school, because the lifestyle and the things I did for the dope just kept me away from school. It was a combination of things. But as I look back at the beginning, a lot of the stuff that I saw and did while I was involved with the gangs gave me a lot of the ideas of things to do to support my habit. If I had enough heart to kick in somebody's house door just to grab a guy that was in there, beat him up, and walk him back outside, what's to prevent me from kicking in that door and robbing everybody in the house? We used to go in the grocery stores and tear up the store and walk out with bags of potato chips and stuff like that. What's the difference between doing that or taking money out of the cash register? Or maybe even robbing everybody else in the store?

It was the need for that dope that just sort of transformed my mind into where I just didn't care. In the beginning it was petty robberies. We used guns, but mainly for show. At that point, I really wasn't prepared to shoot anybody. But I would have a gun on me. So it was little robberies— barber shops, kids we knew had money, grocery stores, little candy stores. A lot of them were fronts for numbers runners, too, but we sort of stayed away from them in the beginning because they would shoot back. And the people who were controlling the numbers knew who was doing what. And they weren't afraid to get retribution. We didn't do a hell of a lot of stickups because, again, to support your habit wasn't really that expensive and I was never really criminal-minded in the sense that I liked crime. I didn't. But the dope was telling me I needed money. So I had to do what I knew how to do.

I committed my first robbery when I was fifteen years old. I had just become involved with drugs to the point where I knew that I had to start doing something different than just get money from my mother and other little odds and ends. I had to really start making some money to pay for my habit. I had gotten together with three other guys and we decided that we were going to rob taxi cabs, since that was the easiest thing besides a store. So all four of us got together and we went up to 163rd Street. We were really sort of like the Three Stooges. We tried to figure out how to stop a taxi cab— how a whole bunch of fifteen-year-old black kids were going to get a taxi cab to stop for us. So we played around with this for about maybe twenty minutes, and we finally decided one of us would stop the cab and then the rest of us would get in the cab. After a while, this is exactly what happened.

I forgot who it was that stopped the cab, but the cab stopped and the rest of us piled in. Before all this happened on this particular day, though, I had gone shopping and I had spent twenty dollars on this brand-new hat, which I had on at the time. So we all got in the cab and it was like a cartoon: all of us are giving the cab driver different directions. We finally settled on one direction. All of us had guns, and we were driving for maybe a quarter of a mile. Then Charles, who was sitting in front, gives us the eye signal: Ok, we're going to do it. Charles tells the driver, "Pull over! Pull over! Pull over!" The cab driver's scared. He looks behind and he looks on the side and he sees all these guns. He starts to pull

25

the cab over to the side of the curb, and Charles says, "Yo man, where's the money? Give up the money!" And the cab driver tells us, well, he just came out, so he really doesn't have any money. At that time cab drivers used to keep all their money in a cigar box, and we all knew that, so we wanted to see. We grabbed the cigar box and there was nothing in it.

In the meantime, the traffic is still going by and people are honking their horns. Either they don't see what's going on or they don't care. We've got the cab driver over to the side and he doesn't have any money in the box. So now you've got four young kids with guns; everybody wants to beat him up, take off his clothes, and tear up the cab to find some money. We know there's some money in this cab. There's got to be some money in this cab—this is a robbery! We turn the box inside out. We turn the cab inside out; there's no money. The cab driver had four dollars of his personal money in his pocket. We took that. Everybody's stumbling around trying to put their guns away, and we're all caught up in the excitement of the moment. We start running like we just committed a major crime and we're running in four different directions. As I'm running I lost my brand new hat. So we just keep running and running and running and finally I get away. Everybody's heart is beating fast. We just did our first major crime—for a grand total of four dollars! It was a fiasco. A fumbling, bumbling fiasco. And later on when I thought about it, if that cab driver had been able to identify any one of us, I would be doing twenty-five years to life for robbery and attempted homicide. It was ridiculous.

Thinking back, I was scared, but this is where peer pressure comes in, I guess. You know, you can't show fear in front of the guys. Either you're down or you're not down. And if you're not down, you can't hang out. In other words, if you're committed to doing whatever it is the fellas are doing—if you're part of the group—this is what you have to do. You've got to commit to the group, whatever they decide to do. And usually in those circumstances and in groups like that, there's always a leader. And if you're not the leader, then you have to be down, you have to be committed. And usually the leader, as part of exercising his control, will have us do stupid things, which happens sometimes.

Leadership of our group fluctuated, because the leader was whoever came up with an idea to do something. And we would either be hanging out together and somebody would come up with an idea and say, "Well, hey man, let's rob this place," or let's rob that, or let's do this or let's do that. And we'll say, "Yeah, okay, let's do it." In the group of guys that I hung out with, after a while the leadership role sort of settled into one person. And this is when I walked away from the group, because I don't like being led around like that. But in the beginning, I would do that, and I guess that's indicative of what most kids my age in my situation go through. I knew what I was doing was wrong, but it was exciting. I knew the penalty if I got caught, but I really didn't care. You know, I didn't think about that. It's just like my drug life, I guess. I knew what it would do, but it was not going to happen to me.

THE FIRST DRUG I EVER SOLD was marijuana. I was about sixteen years old. I was living in the Bronx and going to high school at the time, and I knew Larry, who was one of the older guys on the block. When I met Larry I really didn't know what he did, except I used to see a lot of women around his house all the time so I figured he was into women in some kind of way, but I really didn't know much about it until later on. Larry was a hustler and he was from the South. He sold hot TVs, drugs, women—he sold everything. I went to Larry one day to buy a nickel bag of reefer, and at first, he didn't want to sell it because it was just a five dollar bag. But he finally sold it to me and he sat me down in his house and talked to me a little bit. I guess he was picking my mind, picking my brain. I didn't really understand what all that was about at the time, and he would let me buy a small amount of reefer from him. He was selling lots of keys [kilos] of reefer and he didn't want to get into that street shit of selling nickel bags, but he would let me buy. I would have to come by myself and I'd have to call him first.

I started selling marijuana before I started selling heroin. In fact, I got Larry into selling dope, because he wouldn't touch it before. He always used to keep good reefer, which is why I went to him. Eventually Larry just sat me down one day and told me he liked my style and he liked the way I handled myself and that I could make a lot of money. And that he was going to put me on to some ways of making some money. I used to deliver packages for Larry. I never knew what was in the packages and I never got paid by the people that I delivered the packages to. Larry would always pay me. Well, he always treated me right so I never fucked with the packages or whatever.

One day he told me that since I was buying an awful lot of nickel bags from him, if I had a clientele he would set me up. So I eventually got into selling a lot of reefer. It got to the point where I was selling keys of reefer. I had customers all over New Jersey, lower Manhattan—a lot of hippies, because pot was the thing they liked. Larry would sell me a key of reefer for $250. I sold the key for $400 or $500. And it got to the point where I stopped selling ounces, quarter ounces, quarter pounds, and half pounds because I had such a good key business going.

Larry lived around the corner in a private house at the time. So I would set up my buy, get my money up front, and I'd have the people wait at my house. I'd go around the corner, I'd give Larry his money, I'd take my money and stash it. I mean, I would leave it there with Larry. I'd say, "Here, man, this is your money, this is my money." But I'd have my customer upstairs and I didn't want him to see me dealing with this money. Because my customers were mainly in their twenties and thirties they had the money to buy bulk. And they smoked a lot of reefer. They would come to my house so my mother knew, but she didn't know to what extent I was involved because most of the reefer crowd were okay. They weren't rowdy and they were different from the dope crowd. And my mother's only concern was that I would spend my money right instead of spending it on dope and dumb shit. You see, reefer was a nice drug. Reefer wasn't considered a bad drug.

With all that money I was making I bought clothes and I traveled. I went to Puerto Rico, I'd go down South, and I'd go out West. I started buying clothes from Layton's and Phil Cromfeld clothing stores, the same places that the Rat Pack—Joey Bishop, Frank Sinatra, Sammy Davis, Jr— bought their clothes. I used to buy alpaca knit sweaters, silk pants, alligator shoes—four hundred dollars a pair—I had six or seven pairs of gators. I was sixteen years old and my heroes were Willie Sutton, gangsters like James Cagney, Edward G. Robinson, you know, the tough guys. I used to like all of those movies like *Superfly, Black Caesar, Across 110th Street* and *Angels with Dirty Faces*. And I wanted to be Superfly. I used to buy flamboyant, outrageous clothes. I had a place in Greenwich Village that I used to go to that sold one-of-a-kind unique clothes. And that's where I used to buy them. I used to wear outrageous colors and everything.

Clothes were important because they made me. They showed people outside what I was about. Clothes, jewelry—I sort of got used to having a flashy appearance. After a while—after I got into making money and doing other things—I sort of toned down the way I dressed because I didn't want people to really know what I was doing. But in the beginning, the young guys could just look at me and think, "Man, this dude is cool, this dude is fly—he's got it!" I flashed a lot of money and I spent a lot of money. And I was creating an image. I liked it, I enjoyed it. Because people didn't know me; they knew what I wanted them to know about me. And all I wanted them to know was that I was *somebody*. Because I had money and I had clothes and I had heart. I wanted people to respect me and know that I wasn't a chump. You know, that's all that was really important to me. I was in school at the time and my teachers used to bug out, because I'd come to school dressed with clothes more expensive than they wore. And they couldn't understand that.

Eventually, Larry got into selling dope. And then eventually he got into using dope and then he wasn't paying as much attention to his business enterprises as he was previously. Last I heard, he had gotten busted twice but he had gotten out of jail and I heard he went back down South.

I DROPPED OUT OF HIGH SCHOOL, but at that point it was mostly due to my addiction to drugs. I was in the twelfth grade when I dropped out. Six more months and I could have graduated. Eventually, I ended up getting a GED. My earliest remembrances of school were when I was in Harlem. I enjoyed school. I liked the variety of learning different things and different subjects. I had good grades up until high school in all my classes. Even when I moved up to the Bronx, things like joining the gangs, using alcohol – I really didn't want to get into that because my head was into school things. But I couldn't afford a reputation of being an egghead. Because I had style and other things, and it seems like I was an aberration because I also liked school and I liked the academic subjects. People didn't respect brains, they respected brawn, and I had to have respect. So I had to go out and do these tough-guy things and my heart really wasn't in it. I didn't want to be involved in a gang. But I didn't want to have to deal with fighting the world, my friends included. The few people that I knew that were academically where I was at were spread around the city. And I didn't have a friend who was academically on the same level as I was. So the only way I got that nourishment was in school. I was in a special progress class in sixth grade so I was assigned to this special junior high school. I went through junior high in two years instead of three. All my teachers encouraged me to go further in my education. But I fought it, because my peer group was telling me, forget about education; education ain't going to do this, ain't going to do that. I was even correcting people's speech back then. " 'Ain't' ain't in the dictionary" and this and that. But they couldn't relate to that. So I had to put on my hat backwards in order for me just to fit in.

The teachers always encouraged me. The white guidance counselors were the ones that gave me the problems, because they were locked into the stereotypes about blacks and Hispanics. Some of my teachers were white, some black, especially in South Bronx. Even in Harlem the teachers were black but the administration was white – guidance counselors, principals, assistant principals. And I was always being put into certain categories by the counselors, but the teachers always knew I didn't belong in that category. This is how the counselors would hear about it: "Well, so and so recommended that I talk to you and review your record. Well, you do have a different record, but . . ." and they would always keep me in a group of people who academically I just didn't fit with, people who were at a remedial level. So those classes started to disinterest me, because I was way ahead of them. I would go to the counselor and I would have to beef with him and beef with him to make a change. When I graduated junior high school I was supposed to go to the Bronx High School of Science. Based on my academics, I had already qualified to go there. But there's an entrance exam for the Bronx High School of Science, which I would have had no problem passing. But my junior high school counselor didn't tell me that there was an exam and when the exam date was. In fact, I had to go tell my counselor about the exam. Then she tells me, "Oh, I wasn't aware that there was an exam. I'll find out." She comes back the next day and tells me, "Well, the exam was three weeks ago so we won't be able to get you in." I was real pissed at that. That started my road out of the school system.

The second-highest academically rated high school in New York was Peter Stuyvesant, but since I didn't live in that school district I couldn't go there, so I had to take number three, which was William Howard Taft, which was a piece of cake. And it was boring. I wasn't challenged. And I began to cause trouble in school.

One time I had this hookey party at my house and they sent the paddy wagons over there. While the police were filling up the paddy wagons, we still had the music going—it was like a dance contest. They fill up one paddy wagon, they come in, tap people on the shoulder, you know, you come off the dance floor, you go downstairs, you go to the paddy wagon. I'd come to school drunk or high or I wouldn't come to school at all. I'd fight, I'd yell, I'd argue. I wouldn't do anything right, nothing, till finally I couldn't take it anymore.

I even got into sports because I was bored: pole vaulting, high jumping, high diving—I mean, these are sports you usually don't get into in a concrete school on 171st Street and Grand Concourse in the Bronx. We used to have a little pit in the backyard of the school that we used for pole vaulting. And I excelled in track. And I used to go to the YMCA for high diving. I was so bored, man. All my teachers—all of them—told me, "Listen, just come to school to take the exams. We know you don't want to come to school but come and take

31

the exams; you've got six months and we'll get you out of here."

I guess my mother dealt with a lot of frustration, things that I couldn't see at the time. I was beginning to not only cut classes in school but also I was getting deeper into my drug habit and getting into trouble. And my mother always tried to have something for us, like a sort of middle-class way of living in a lower-class neighborhood. We were never rich, not anywhere near it, but the apartments and the projects where we lived were always decent. My mother worked for the phone company all her life. She started as an operator. When she died of cervical cancer at age fifty-one, she was an area supervisor. When my mother first discovered I was involved with a group that was getting into trouble, she used to curse me out. My mother always knew I was academically capable, and she couldn't understand why I would choose to be with a certain segment of the population as opposed to people she felt were my academic peers.

3

STICKUPS, BURGLARIES AND RIP-OFFS

EVERY PLACE THAT THE DEALERS congregated to sell drugs there were always drug addicts. Informal hangout places. So every morning at the start of the day I would go to one of these spots whether I had money or not. And there was always somebody there who had a heist or something planned or who had an idea of a way to make money. And I was like a jack-of-all-trades—I was open to anything that would make some money. I would go down to one of the places if I had some money and I would buy a couple of bags. I would talk to a guy who sold it and he would tell me what he's got going, and I'd say, "Okay, wait a minute. Let me go get straight." And I would go shoot up, I would get high, and I would come back and then do whatever it was he had in mind: like robberies, for instance. When I would come and hang out, sometimes I had a gun, sometimes I didn't. Most of the time I really didn't carry a weapon. There was a time when I was heavy into weapons but it was a very short period. Usually if they had an idea, they had a weapon or knew where I could go get another weapon. Guns invite trouble. I know it sounds crazy, but most of the time if you pull a gun, you're going to have to use a gun. When I was first

33

into it, it was like all you had to do was show the gun and that was enough to scare people. But then as the robberies and violence kept going on, you almost had to pretend you were going to shoot them to get them to do whatever you wanted. I don't know, maybe I was thinking about the easy way out but I just never really felt comfortable with that.

One night I was by myself and I had just gotten high and I had some money; matter of fact, I really didn't want to go on the robbery, but I ran into a friend of mine, Alvin. And he needed another man—a wheel man—and I always had a car. So we went to this Kentucky Fried Chicken in the Bronx and they tell me about it on the way over. I had no idea where we were going or what we were going to do. All I knew was that we were going to stick up a joint. So I drove Alvin and another guy. I parked the car in the middle of a wide-split street, and Kentucky Fried Chicken was around the corner. Just before we got out of the car Alvin gave me a gun. We went inside and there were two customers and one guy behind the counter. Alvin grabbed the guy behind the counter and he stuck the gun to his head. I took the two customers and pushed them to the side and held the gun on them; the other guy just stood by the door. Alvin jumped over the counter and made the guy give up the money out of the safe, and threatened him, which was standard: don't call the police, don't use the phone, don't touch the alarm, or anything.

We stayed in there for a total of maybe three minutes; we got the money and ran out. When we got to my car it wouldn't start. So here we are with a stickup around the corner and the cops are starting to come now; but they're coming off of the big avenue, off the boulevard, and they're coming in that way. The guy must have tripped an alarm inside. This was all right, because we understood that there was a possibility that would happen, but again at that point, depending upon the situation . . . I know Alvin—if Alvin was mad he might have shot the guy who triggered the alarm. But the primary thing was getting the money.

The car wouldn't start so the two of them are in the back and they're sweating and laughing at the same time. I don't know if they were high, because they had just shot some drugs before we went on the heist. But, see, at that point when you get involved in drugs you have to shoot drugs at least one time to get straight. Just so you can be normal, stop the shakes and everything. Getting high at that point—unless you got the money, you can't even worry about that. So I would say that Alvin and his partner were straight. I was half-assed high. It was like a dream to me; I wasn't rushing or anything. I didn't really care at that point. I had a gun in my pocket so I was ready to shoot it out.

When we ran out of the Kentucky Fried Chicken they saw what general direction we ran in, but nobody saw us running to the car, which was a bright, canary yellow Cutlass Supreme. When we got in the car, they're laying down in the back and I'm trying to crank up the engine and it wouldn't crank. So I had to get out of the car and go under the hood: the wires were wet. I had to play with the wires for a little while, but I got back in the car, got it started, and pulled out into the avenue. The store was maybe twenty-five feet away. The squad cars are pulling in. I stopped, waited for the red light, made the right turn and we drove home. We split up the money, bought some more dope, and went upstairs. We got about $2,700 out of that. And that was a big haul for an off-the-top-of-your-head stickup.

I was involved in two bank stickups in Brooklyn, but I didn't plan that. They called me at the last minute. It was kind of scary. The banks were small, community mini-banks. There were only maybe three people in the bank: two tellers and a person to handle inquiries or whatever. To this day I still don't know how we didn't get caught. Again, before we went down, I just got straight, not high, and I needed the money. This was like a turning point in my life, because I had decided that robbery was going to be one of the tools that I was going to use to make some money. And again, it might sound crazy: I don't really like violence and I don't like shooting people and I don't like really threatening people, but when I need dope all that goes out the window. I never did like sticking up grocery stores. I've been with guys a few times that stuck up grocery stores and I didn't have a gun and I didn't know it was going to be a robbery. I went out with some crazy guys. They just told me, "Listen, park the car right here and we'll go get some cigarettes." And the next thing I know people are running out the store and they're yelling, "He's got a gun in his hand," and we'd drive away. But I couldn't see doing these kinds of robberies, because the people in the grocery stores work hard for their money, and they have to deal with enough problems every day. And at that time I was reading in the papers about people getting killed for four dollars, ten dollars, fifteen dollars, twenty dollars—it just didn't make sense to me in a weird kind of way.

So after Pablo told me about these banks that they were going to do in Brooklyn, we did them both in the same day. I was kind of, I wouldn't say scared, as much as I was thrilled at that point, because I had made up my mind I was going to stick up the bank. You had to make a decision whether you were going to do it or not. Up until then I had a few gas station stickups, one or two. My main thing was numbers spots. I used to stick up numbers spots all the time. So I went through this fantasy from TV, you know, this big caper holding up a bank. And we're thinking about the Feds coming in and big shoot-outs and this and that. Two of the guys that I was with on the job were really crazy. I think they really wanted to get caught or get involved in a shoot-out. But I just wanted to be expedient; I wanted to go in and get the money and get the hell out. And luckily that's what happened. We had masks on and there were three of us and a driver outside, and we went in the bank. Pablo and I hopped over the counter—this was before the plexiglass and before they were spraying money with a chemical to help identify stolen bank money and everything. We emptied out the cash drawers and one of the guys had a gun on the lady that was sitting down at the desk. He was holding her, but she was kind of fidgety and nervous. I kept looking over, because I had a funny feeling that he was going to shoot her if the lady panicked or something; not that she was going to press the alarm but she'd never been involved in a bank holdup before. And I was more worried about that than getting caught or anything else.

Again, I was fortunate, because in these two bank robberies there was no violence—well, there was violence in the second one; we had to pistol-whip a lady who was running off at the mouth, but there was no shooting, stabbing, other things. So we jumped over the counter and I can remember thinking about him harming the lady and I was thinking about spending the money. I wasn't worried about the cops being outside. I wasn't worried about an alarm. I was taking money out of the drawers and sticking it in the bags. We got $17,000 and some change from that job.

I've done a lot of stickups with a weapon. I never knew personally the people that I robbed, so there was never a relationship built up. To me they were just objects. I never shot anybody that I robbed. I never really violently hurt anybody that I robbed. There were instances where I had to shoot someone to discipline them but that was an occupational hazard—one of my runners, one of my dope dealers. But I didn't develop any type of attachment toward the people that I robbed. It was the dope that was telling me: *get the money.* So I really didn't have time or energy to think about what these people felt or what they thought. Because I was living for three things: getting money to buy dope to get high. Nothing else in my life came in between those three things. I didn't care about anything or anybody except getting money to buy dope to get high.

We used to stick up numbers parlors because that's where the money was. Or we would stick up dope dealers because they also had money. We'd try to find one who was in a secluded spot, either in a hallway or an alleyway, even in an apartment. And by that time I was getting a reputation: "That guy's crazy, leave him alone." A lot of times when people used to see me coming down the street they would stop dealing. I tried to pick and choose most of the people that I stuck up. I didn't really want to mess with somebody who was in a big type of organization or who I knew was dealing for somebody that I knew. There were many times guys came looking for me but they didn't know where I lived. Since I lived in the Bronx, we would go take off some dealers maybe in Brooklyn, Queens, lower Manhattan or a different part of the Bronx. People would get upset and they would look for you for a while, but having your dealer stuck up or even having them rob you was an occupational hazard. We never really got a whole lot of money sticking up low-level drug dealers. The most we ever got off them was a couple hundred and a lot of dope.

One time I went to this dope house in Manhattan. It was in black Harlem. We got inside the apartment and there were maybe four people there. One with a shotgun, the guy who's dealing dope and two others. There were two of us that went in and we had miscounted because we thought there were only two people in there. And when we went in these guys let us in; they patted us down but they didn't find the guns. I had one in the small of my back, a nine millimeter, and they just patted you down quickly and went ahead and took care of business. So while I was buying the dope, my partner was by the door and didn't see the other two guys that were in the apartment. Apartments in Harlem are misleading, because there's a lot of rooms in them. And some of the doors you might think are closets are really rooms. When I went into the living room to buy the dope, the guy had all this dope sitting here and he had all this money stacked up over there. So when he came in, I put the gun to his head and told him it was a stickup. He looked at me and laughed, so I pushed him back in his chair and I started grabbing money and stuffing it in my pocket. Then I hear all this yelling: "Yo man, it's a stickup, it's a stickup! Move! There he is— in the blue shirt." Pow! Pow! Pow!

Bullets whizzed by my head, and I looked inside. My man was crouched down in the hall. He was sitting down and I thought he was shot but he wasn't. He just shot at the bodyguard at the door. The bodyguard ran in the room and closed the door. But then another door opened in between me and the door, and two guys came running out of there with guns in their hands and they started firing at me. And the guy who was dealing dope—the one that I stuck up— was reaching for a gun; so I cracked him on the side of his head with the butt of the gun and I took his gun from him. I saw that these guys were between me and the door and my man was still crouched down on the floor, but he was holding the guy across from him at bay with the gun and he looked like a little insect. All that the guys in the hall could shoot at were his legs; and for some miraculous reason they missed. But he had two guns, so he was holding this one guy over here with one gun and firing the other gun sporadically down the hall. Then I told him, "Yo man, open the door." He got the apartment door open, and once he did that I ran from where I was. It was like a gauntlet, because the two guys were right there. I just ran up the hall firing and ran out the door and my man came behind me.

When I got outside I fired a few more shots down the hall. And my partner ran out and we ran outside. We ran for about three miles. It was difficult because it was a dope fiend neighborhood. Everybody heard the gunshots and they knew what was happening. When we came running out the building there were people standing in our way. I don't know if they were scared to shoot or what. But we just pushed them out of the way and we started running. And then the other guys came downstairs and they're shooting at us. Morris Park was across the street, and we ran into the park. Ran over to Park Avenue and over to the west side of Manhattan. And then we ran across the bridge into the grass . . . and we got away.

I USED TO HAVE A FEMALE crime partner, Terese, who was bisexual. But she was one of the best stickup partners that I ever worked with. We also had sex once in a while, but she preferred women. She was an addict—she'd shoot up—but it was on like a different level. It wasn't an all-the-time dope fiend type thing. She used to dress up, she used to go out, she used to party. Her old lady used to work in an administrative position in one of the hospitals, and she used to live with this girl on 102nd Street.

We stuck up a numbers joint one night. And Terese and I walked in the joint. Terese had two pistols, I had two pistols, and she smacked the shit out of this dude that was at the door. I mean she just cold-cocked him. She turned around and said, "Everybody empty your pockets. I don't want to see nothing move but the money. The first motherfucker to reach for anything but money I'm going to blow his head off." That was it. We also stuck up a couple of other numbers joints and dope dealers. It was like clockwork. Terese would do one thing, I would do another thing, but it was together. It was like we were reading each other's minds. We did great. Eventually I got busted on another robbery, Terese went to a drug program, and we sort of got away from it.

I KNEW GUYS WHO WERE PICKS—did things like picking locks, getting in apartments. I wasn't really that sophisticated. I was probably what you call a smash-and-go burglar. I'd smash the window, stick my hand through there and turn the door-knob. One time I was in the South Bronx, and arbitrarily I had picked this apartment. It was on the eighth floor. I had tried to go in through the door, but the opening was too small and I couldn't get my hand in, but I did get a peek inside the apartment and it looked pretty decent, so I figured there was something in there. And I didn't want to give it up, so I went up on the roof and I traced it, you know, like from where the apartment was to which window would fit going inside the apartment. I didn't have any rope or equipment or anything and it's a straight drop all the way down; there's nothing to hold on to. So I was trying to figure out a way to get over the side of the roof and get in the window.

There was a thin TV antenna wire. I figured I'd hold onto that to lower myself down to the window and then go in through the window. I don't know what possessed me to do that. Anyway, I climbed over the side of the roof and looked down. There's no fire escape; there's nothing, just a straight drop. Eight stories, straight down. So I climbed over the side, and the window was, I would say, maybe eight to ten feet from the top of the roof. I climbed over and here I am hanging by my arms and my foot is just barely touching the top of the windowsill. I needed to come down a little further but the window ledge wasn't wide enough for me to chance jumping because at the end there was nothing to hold on to. So I hit upon this bright idea: I would hold on to this thin brown TV antenna cord and lower myself down. I held onto the wire and, at that point, it felt pretty strong, but when I let go my weight, of course, it started to bring the wire down. It's a thin piece of plastic wire. Two thin wire connections. At the same time the wire broke and I started to fall, I got a toehold in the top of the window, which was locked from the inside. There were maybe six inches of open space and then there was another lock on it. My foot caught on that open space and my body weight falling is what broke the lock.

I ended up straddling the window. And as the TV wire fell, I watched it go down eight stories. I had my left leg hooked over the window and I'm looking down; and the wire's going all the way down—and it could have been me. So eventually I just grabbed on because my leg was hooked over both windows now and I went into the apartment. There wasn't a lot of money, maybe one hundred twenty dollars in cash and a lot of camera equipment and stuff, so I took all that and on my way out of the apartment I discover that it's a double cylinder lock. And there's no key in the lock. So then I had to spend another half an hour looking for a goddamn screwdriver so I could take the lock off the door.

When I got downstairs I had put all this stuff in a brown paper bag. It took me almost three hours to get rid of those cameras, you know, because everybody wants to give you five dollars. I got a diamond—five dollars. I got a gold watch—five dollars. They know you're a junkie; they know you're strung out. They know you have some good quality stuff and they know people are not willing to pay; and I didn't want to take the time to go to my fence because I was in a strange neighborhood and I wanted to get out right away. People knew it was hot and they bought it. As long as it wasn't theirs, they didn't care. They were getting a deal. A five hundred dollar camera for fifty dollars, seventy-five dollars, one hundred dollars. They'd give it up. And a strange thing happened: after I got rid of all the cameras and stuff, I thought about what I had just done. And my body started shaking and that whole picture came to my mind. In fact, I lived with that picture every time I went to sleep at night for about a week or two. I wondered what possessed me to hold onto a thin antenna wire—to think that it was going to hold me going over the roof. It was fate. I don't know, people used to call me *el Gato*, because I had nine lives. I mean, I should be dead right now from half the shit I did, like that burglary and a bunch of other stuff.

The burglary that I did get busted for was in Yonkers. I was due. I was overdue, because I was burning this neighborhood up everyday. I was only getting two or three hundred dollars a burglary and it just wasn't enough money to support my habit, which was a good four or five hundred dollars a day. So there I was back in the same neighborhood doing the same thing every day. Smashing goddamn door windows to get into the house. I was waiting until I really got sick before I bought dope. At this point I really wasn't getting high; I was just getting straight, you know, just to stay normal. There was no getting high at this point.

It was a rainy day and I did it again: smashed a door window, opened the door, went in, closed the door and locked it. As I passed a doorway on the way upstairs, I thought I saw somebody else and it startled me because I thought somebody was home. I stopped and said, "Oh shit," and I looked and it was a mirror, just my reflection in an alcove. I kept hearing a dog bark, too, and I saw a light on downstairs. But I had banged on the door and nobody was home. So I get upstairs and I spent about fifteen to twenty minutes in the house. I kept finding little pieces of jewelry here and there—gold, rings, chains—and about one hundred dollars in cash. I had a pocketful of jewelry, but for some reason I wasn't really satisfied. I started looking around the other bedrooms and then an alarm kept going off in my head: you're spending too much time in this house—get out now. But because I only had like a hundred dollars in cash, I'm looking for more money. And that's what did me in, because I spent all that time in the house.

I walked out the house the same way I came in. I walked downstairs and in front of the house I make a left turn like I'm going towards the train station. And then I hear someone shout, "Halt!" I turn around and a half a block away two cops are pointing guns at me. I start running and that's when they started shooting. There's a trainyard right there so I ran into the trainyard and they chased me. In the meantime, I'm starting to get rid of all the evidence. I'm throwing money out of my pocket, throwing jewelry away and everything. I run through the trainyard and I come out a different entrance. And as I was running out of the entrance toward the street I ran right into the cop. He had a gun at my head. The other cops came and threw me on the ground. I had guns in my ears, my nose, my eyes, guns everywhere. They handcuffed me, threw me in the back of the car, and took me to the precinct. That's when they started dropping all the rest of these burglaries on me. I was careless; I didn't wear gloves, no mask, nothing—just smashed in the goddamn window, opened the door and went in. So we worked out a deal: if I would confess to all those burglaries, plus some unsolved burglaries that they had so they could close the books, they would recommend probation if I went into a drug program. And that's what happened. I went into a drug program and I walked away from all that shit.

I've committed hundreds of burglaries in my lifetime but was arrested for burglary only that one time. And then I copped out to burglaries that I didn't even do. But it was paperwork. It was a deal. You know, it made their job easy. They didn't have to deal with people and leave the books open. So I copped out; it didn't give me more time so I didn't care. I'd have copped out to murder, man, and walked away.

IN 1976 I WAS TWENTY-NINE years old and living with my common-law wife, Lois. She knew I was robbing places. But she didn't say anything—she was scared because we had just had a daughter at the time. My wife was also scared for me because she didn't want me to get hurt and I couldn't understand that. I ended up blowing the marriage. We stayed together maybe three and a half, four years before I got locked up. And then I was away from her for about two years. At the time I was doing the robberies she understood that she couldn't control me, but I was expected, in a sense, to just respect the house. Don't bring that shit home. Don't have people come into the house looking for me—wanting to do harm to me, her, or my daughter. So I did that to the best of my knowledge, the best of my ability. There was one time when I had to go out and hurt a guy because he came to my house looking for me, and I came home that night and my wife was scared to death. I asked her what happened. She took about a half hour and finally told me. So I went up Southern Boulevard and I caught the dude and I pistol-whipped him out in the street. I was going to blow his brains out but another dope fiend that I knew had come up behind me and said, "No, man, don't do that."

I had stuck him and his partner up; they were dealing dope and I had robbed him and they found out where I lived. It was one of the times, you know, when you need money; you don't really have time to plan these robberies. A lot of

times you might not have a car or you might not be motivated to go all the way downtown, far away from your neighborhood. So you go not too far from where you live.

I lived in the black ghetto, and the surrounding neighborhoods were black and Hispanic, but the people that I went to
rob, except for some dope dealers, were people with money
in other areas of the city. As far as burglaries were concerned,
I usually went to affluent white neighborhoods. I've broken
into apartments in my own neighborhood, but they ain't got
shit in the house: an old black and white TV, no jewelry, a
camera maybe, a checkbook or two. Nonproductive.

Being dark-skinned, I always wanted to go in quick and
come out quick in white neighborhoods. And I would go at
odd hours, like early in the morning or in the afternoon when
there were a lot of people around so I would blend in. Every
time I went out I never looked like a bum so people couldn't
say, well, this dirty guy came in the neighborhood and we
followed him up there. And most of the time I had a car,
which I would leave parked somewhere else. So I would only
be in that neighborhood for a little while. I mean, you always
had time to do whatever it is you were going to do before
the cops came and people said anything. But you would have
to use that time wisely.

As you go further up in the Bronx, there are private
houses; there are no more tall tenement buildings. Certain
neighborhoods are laid out a little more like a bunch of private houses grouped together. I remember I started out one
morning and I had seen this area a couple of times in the
past, so I decided I was going to burglarize this neighborhood. In fact I took the train up there and I walked around
a little bit. In this part of the Bronx it's not unusual to see
a black person since black people live in the neighborhood.
But they are considered upper-middle class because they
could afford a house. So it wasn't strange to see a black person walking around the neighborhood, or a Hispanic person. It was strange to see a bum.

I did my thing: I knocked on the door real hard. I rang
the doorbell. I banged on the door real hard just to make
sure nobody answered. It was eight o'clock in the morning.
I figured everybody had gone to work; they had already left.

You have to be at work at 9:00, so if you live in that part of the Bronx, you have to leave at the latest about 7:30. I listened a little bit, looked around, and smashed the window. I open the door and the chain is on from the inside. So right away that should have told me somebody's in the house. But I thought, well, maybe they left through the side door or the back door, because I really wanted to go in the house and get some money so I could get out. I didn't want any interruptions or obstacles in my way. I didn't want to believe that someone was home. I took the chain off and I went inside. I'm starting to walk up the stairs and this girl comes walking out of this room and she says: "You got to get out of my house right now. What are you doing here?" She was a teenager, about seventeen, eighteen years old and I was scared to death, because a few things went through my head like rape, or just tie her up anyway, and this and that, but none of that made sense to me. Tie her up for what? There might not even be any money in here; then I have these people looking for me not only for burglary, but for assault and anything else that might happen. For burglary, man, it isn't worth it, so I gave her some bullshit line that I got the wrong house, that I was looking for so and so and I gave her some phony name. And she repeated: "Well, nobody's home; I think you should leave right now." She didn't get too close, but she stood her ground. I told her I'm sorry and I walked out of the house.

I left the neighborhood. Well, not really. I went a little further down. You get crazy in those days. You figure you walk a couple of blocks away, but the police precinct covers the whole district, the whole neighborhood, and I figured I'd walk a couple of blocks and nobody would be the wiser. I wasn't getting rich doing burglaries up there, but it was productive: two hundred, three hundred dollars. One time I got nine hundred dollars. I got into a place and the doors were locked and I couldn't smash my way in. But for some reason I wanted to get into this house. So I went around the back and the doors were closed but there was an open window on the second floor. But there's no way to get up to the second floor. So I looked around the back and took a ladder out of the neighbor's yard. I put the ladder up to the window

45

and broke in the house. I'm in the bedroom and I'm looking through the drawers and closet and stuff. I'm pissed off at first because all I'm finding is slum jewelry, you know, fake gold-filled junk, and no money. So I open the closet door and I'm looking through the pockets of clothes; I'm looking in the bottom of the closet. I reach the top shelf—bingo! I hit this little grey tin box. By looking at it I knew it was a money box, and the key was right there on the shelf. I took the key and cranked the box open. Hundreds, fifties, twenties, tens, fives, ones—it had nine hundred and some odd dollars in it and a couple of gold rings, gold and diamond rings and I took all of it. That was a pretty good haul.

I hired a fence, a Cuban guy that used to own a joyeria, a Spanish jewelry store, in the South Bronx. I would take him all my jewelry and he would pay; he knew it was hot. He would weigh it and he would pay for the gold by the penny weight. He would examine the stones and we would dicker over the prices. It was a jewelry store. But when I came in, if he had customers there, I would go back out. As he got to know me, he would tell me to come on in and have a seat, because, again, I was clean; so when I walked into the jewelry store it wasn't like I was a bum and I was going to steal. I had worked up to get this relationship because when I first started burglarizing I was coming up with all these goods. I used to go to a lot of different joints in New York that buy gold and jewelry. I would never give them my ID but I would go to a couple of them and then I would go back to the one that gave me the fairest price. Eventually they tried to jerk you off because they knew what you were doing. From my personal experience, I would say that a number of jewelry shops in New York City are also fences on the side. It was easy for them to take gold, melt it down and renumber it. The stones they put in another setting. I mean, hey man, that's money.

WHEN I WAS SHOOTING DOPE there were times when I also had legitimate jobs that provided opportunities to steal money. I used to work in the garment district. I pushed racks for the garment transfer company—a trucking firm—from the factories that manufactured clothes. They would send us off to the manufacturing joints with one or two empty racks to go pick up the clothes and bring them back. Once we got up into those clothing factories they would count the clothes and put them on the garment rack. But as soon as they turned their back, we'd snatch anything that was close by. The only problem was how to stash all of the dresses and stuff that you stole. So we used to have different places between the manufacturer and the trucking company where we would stash the extra stuff. And at the end of the day we'd be riding the train home with boxes full of clothes. We took them back to the neighborhoods and sold them: brand new dresses, top quality coats, furs, leathers.

One of the sweetest jobs I ever had was working for the city down on Church Street. I used to work in the main computer room where they printed the welfare checks, which were then sent to a mail room where they would store them. They had machines in the mail room that used to put the checks in envelopes with glassed-in fronts with the person's name and address showing through. They'd store the checks in file cabinets to be put in mail bags and sent out two days before check day. While I was in the Job Corps I had learned computer programing so I got hired as a low-level computer person in the mail room.

The first thing that blew my mind was the fact that I was surrounded by all of these checks. This is where all the welfare checks for the entire city were kept. I couldn't believe it. There was a security guard outside who sort of checked us as we left every day to see if we had taken anything, but he didn't really search you unless he had good reason to. Right away my head started clicking, because I was still using dope. I was working, but I was still strung out. I'd even shoot up in this welfare joint. So one day, I took a couple of checks and brought them to Larry. Larry knew this guy named Buddy, who was into false ID and other things. He was also a low-level dope dealer, but his specialty was mainly checks—a paper man. I worked out an agreement with Larry and Buddy. Two or three days before check day, I would take a bunch of checks out of the mail room and I'd get them up to Buddy. I would wait two or three days until he cashed some of them and then get paid my share. I took Buddy as many checks as he could get cashed. I got a percentage; I didn't care what his expenses were or what he had to do—I wanted half. But I was bringing him so much money that we were all making money.

I worked this scam for about six months. What I didn't know at the time was that Buddy was ripping me off, too. I was so happy to get the checks and the money that I really didn't make a list of the stolen checks and the amounts. He would tell me, well, we only got X amount of dollars this time, or we lost some, you know, all this bullshit. Although I never got caught for stealing checks, I got disillusioned with Buddy, and finally stopped going to work.

I used to get disillusioned quick when I was young and I was working and using dope, because I couldn't see where it was leading; and the money started to dry up. It wasn't enough anymore to support my habit and everything else, so I really started to lose interest. In order for me to keep stealing checks I would have had to find another fence and I really didn't want to go through that at this point. And I didn't have access to phony welfare identifications like Buddy. He also had a group of women that used to go around cashing these checks. This is all they used to do all day long at the check cashing joints—"bust digits" or cash stolen checks. It was a sweet setup. I'd bring the checks and Buddy had the network. But he started ripping me off. He gave me back some checks one day and said, well, he couldn't cash them any more because of some bullshit technicality, but I looked at the checks and I remember I had given him a couple of four hundred, three hundred, and two hundred dollar checks. The only checks I got back were eighty, ninety-one, and one hundred one dollar checks. So I stopped working.

When I came back from the Job Corps in 1967, my first job was working in the computer department of a bank in New York. When I started working I had lied on the application because I had already been busted once, but it had been a while. I liked the job, and I was coming to work every day. And my work was good when I was there. My supervisor called me in three weeks after I had been there and asked me if I liked the job and other things. Then he said he had to ask me some questions. Is this your right address? I said,

"Yeah." Is this your right social security number? I said, "Yeah." He asked if I had ever been arrested. I answered, "No—well—" I was thinking fast on my feet—so I told him I had, but it involved alcohol or something stupid and my lawyer said the charge was dismissed or what have you and if I'm ever asked by an employer, I should tell him no. So my supervisor bought it. He had already asked some other people that I worked with about how my work was going and this and that.

I really liked working with computers. But I was also still shooting dope. They would pay us by depositing money into our account and give us a checkbook. And every two weeks, you would just write a check for the amount of your salary. I learned how to juggle around that so I began writing checks almost every day. Of course, my account got overdrawn. I lost interest in the job, but I kept taking cabs downtown cashing checks. And as long as they were under a hundred dollars they never checked anything. You'd tell them you were just starting at the bank and show them some ID. The job lasted a few weeks and I burned it out.

Most of the legitimate jobs I had I thought sucked. There wasn't enough money for the effort involved. And I always knew there was an easier way, and after a while I got used to the easier way. I didn't like the constraints of working for a boss. My attitude was that I'll work for you but don't tell me what to do. I couldn't stand anybody giving me orders all the time. And I'd work for a little while and I'd quit. I wanted to be my own boss; I didn't want to have people telling me what to do, what time to come in, and everything else. So it was easier just to leave the working world and be your own boss.

4

CHAPTER

DEALING DOPE

I GOT TIRED OF ROBBING AND stealing and bringing my money to the dope dealers. All these scars and holes I have all over my body—they didn't get any of that. All they get is cash money. A friend of mine and I had gotten together and it was his idea that we start dealing dope ourselves. We managed to have a little money left over from some of the capers that we did. So one day Chico suggested that we have our own drug supply. This way we don't have to keep running out in the street getting busted or ripped off all the time. It was easy to go back up the line to find out who was doing drugs wholesale. Most of the street dealers were more than glad to turn you on to their supplier if it would mean something for them. We would have to go up the ladder one or two notches since the reason for buying drugs in quantity is to save money. So we ended up buying a couple of half-a-loads. A half-a-load is like fifteen two dollar bags, which usually retails for like thirty dollars but if you buy in quantity you can get discounts. I think we were getting halves for something like twenty-three, twenty-five dollars. This was around 1963, 1964 when dope was in two dollar bags, three dollar bags, and five dollar bags. We used to call them pound bags, five dollar pound bags. Eventually the prices started going up.

Chico and I found out who had nice quality dope in Brooklyn and we bought a couple of halves from them. We came back to the Bronx and we told people around the neighborhood that we had some good Brooklyn dope and we were selling it. It was good enough for people to buy it one time and want to come back and buy some more. A lot of times when you're buying dope you get half-ass dope and you're not too enthused about really going back to the same person, unless there's no one else and then you go back to the same person. So we did this for a while off and on. I had a problem with it because Chico was always looking for the money, but I ended up shooting the dope because it was good. I couldn't see holding on to it. Plus my habit had me getting more and more into the dope and Chico was trying to tell me, you know, season it off and try to regulate yourself, but I just could never regulate my dope.

As the word got around the neighborhood that we had good dope and the number of our customers increased, that's when the problems started. That's one of the times I got stuck up. It was on the corner of Trinity Avenue in the Bronx. People were coming up to me and I would take them in the hallway and we would exchange money for dope. Two guys came in one time and at this point I was selling dope to everyone. I really wasn't worried about the cops or anything. I should have been worried about bandits, though. They came in the hall and I asked them how much dope they wanted and they said, "We want it all—give it up." They pulled out guns and they had me back in the hall, and I was scared. The only good thing about it was I had maybe only two halves on me, but I had a lot of money because I had been selling dope all morning, and they took it all. I got pissed off, but I later found out who it was. I went to one of the guy's houses, kicked in the door, and went up to the room. He was hiding in the back room with the other guy. And I pistol-whipped both of them. I took off all their clothes; I took their money; I took the TV, radio and clothes and threw all that stuff out in the street, because I didn't want any of it. I was just pissed off because they stuck me up. I got stuck up a couple of other times after that dealing dope. That's one of the hazards of the business. But that was how I started, anyway, just buying small quantities of heroin. I had a little reputation, and I always managed to get good dope. And dope, like any other good quality product, will sell itself, so I didn't have to run out in the street and try and grab people.

While I was selling dope off and on, I was still robbing and burglarizing, because at that point dope dealing just didn't appeal to me. I was kind of hooked on the lifestyle of the dope fiend and I didn't have the time just to sit there and sell dope for small change. I couldn't see the profit in it, you know, five dollars or ten dollars just wasn't worth it to me. Eventually I ran into this Cuban guy, Tito, who used to be a bus driver for the New York Transit Authority. Tito used to own an after-hours club, too. He had some money and had dope connections but he didn't really care too much about dealing dope since he had so many other things that were making money for him. I was introduced to Tito through this other bus driver that I used to know. We went over to Tito's house one night and he had a lot of brown dope. At this time there were different kinds of dope going under different names like China White and Mexican Brown. The only difference in the color was what you cut it with. People were under the false impression that the brown was more pure. So Tito had this dope in the house for a long time; he only dealt it to his friends and he wasn't really a dope dealer. But the crowd he ran around with were big dope dealers that would come to his house. They would give him dope or Tito would spend fifty dollars on some dope and he would end up with a profit of like five hundred dollars off that fifty dollars.

Anyway, I started dealing for Tito. I just told him to keep the dope coming. I had a couple of spots where I used to sell dope. I tried not to sell it out of my house because I don't want people knocking on my door at three, four, five o'clock in the morning, and dope fiends will do that if they know you have good dope and they get sick. They don't care what time it is, they'll come to your house. At this time I was selling dope out of bars, mainly on St. Ann's Avenue in the Bronx.

When I was selling dope for Tito and Hector, this big time independent dope dealer, as long as I maintained connections with the right people, I'd never have problems with the police. And they knew where I was going when I would come to

Hector's house. I bought dope from him. I would pick up maybe four or five ounces of "pure dope," and the police knew, because there used to be detectives sitting right outside of Hector's house, and they would see me go in and see me leave. And then when I would go to one of my factories and get it cut, they knew who my workers were, because they knew who Hector's workers were. Cops in New York are not stupid. They knew Hector was dealing dope. They knew Tito was dealing dope. But Tito also had an after-hours club downstairs and a lot of Tito's thing was cocaine. Tito deals a lot of cocaine. There were cops, off-duty detectives, that used to come to the after-hours spot and sniff cocaine downstairs. I used to sit at the table sometimes and Tito would bring me around, put his arm around me and introduce me. He'd say, "This is my number one man." Two of the police were in a tactical narcotics unit. Others were detectives and a few were patrolmen. Some in the Bronx. Some in Queens, Yonkers. They bought cocaine from Tito, but the amount of cocaine that they were buying they could not possibly use themselves. So I am surmising that they had their own network.

I worked for Tito for a couple of months until he got disinterested and he cut loose his connections. So I started looking around for some new connections. I had a little bit of a reputation from all the other crazy things that I was doing so I got to know a couple of people; and it surprised me, because most of these people who were into wholesale drugs owned grocery stores, hardware stores, clothing stores, or clubs. And I knew a couple of them because I used to buy my clothes at some of these neighborhood stores. Once you knew what the street hierarchy was, it was very easy to know who was dealing drugs and who wasn't. Most drug dealers get caught up in the flamboyant part of dealing. You know, it was very hard for them to keep cool. They had big cars and fancy clothes and flashed a lot of money and jewelry. You could more or less pick them out. So I ran into a couple of wholesalers at this point who were making good money selling dope. Actually, I wasn't buying anything at this time. They were giving me some dope on consignment, and I just had to give them like twelve dollars off a half-a-load, which meant that I kept more than half the profits for myself. I was still running into trouble with this because I was shooting up a lot of dope. And I would fantasize about how I'll shoot this and when I get the next package from him I'll make it up off of that package. And that got me into trouble quite a few times, because I stopped robbing and stealing but I kept using up all the dope. I would go out in the morning and whatever I didn't sell the first time I'd go back upstairs and I'd shoot it and get high. I was running from dealers like this for about a good eighteen months. I'd use one connection and I'd burn him out and I'd go to another one and I'd burn him out.

EVENTUALLY I SET UP MY OWN distribution operation. I had my own workers, my own couriers. At one time I had about sixty people working for me in Manhattan, Brooklyn, and the Bronx. I had two penthouses, one in the Bronx and one in Manhattan. What I'd do is pick up the drugs—most of the time it was in the Bronx, once or twice it was in Manhattan—I would pick up maybe a quarter pound, or a half pound, or two or three pounds. I'd take it to one of my factories in an apartment and they'd have on surgical masks. At that point when we were cutting dope, you could get high off the fumes. You would end up nodding into the cutting table, so usually I would try to pick people that didn't use dope to work in the factory—neighborhood people that needed money. And I was an equal opportunity employer. I tried to get females, because they'd work and they did a good job. They were money conscious. Men—they get around all that dope and they get greedy.

So from the time I picked up the dope I would take it or I would have it sent from one of my runners to one of the factories. But you lost money all along the line. Everybody would take out a little at every step. But dope was so plentiful and you could make so much off of so little that you just considered that a business expense. We would have tons of lactose, milk, sugar, quinine, benieta, measuring spoons, glassine bags, rubber bands; paper bags to put the dope in after we finished cutting it and everything.

I was about twenty-two or twenty-three years old and was

still using drugs, but I was getting so much dope that I could afford to keep up a different kind of image. I was sort of semi-disciplining myself, because when I was around the tables and my own workers I couldn't show these people that I was still getting high—that I was out of it—because they'd have robbed me blind. So I had people running these houses that I sort of half-trusted, half-intimidated. That's about as much as you can expect. I used to try and be at the two different locations where I had my factories, and I would also have to be out on the street at the dealer level because when I first started I didn't trust anybody with money. I would go around to all my different dealers and I would pick up the money myself until I got hip to the fact that you can get busted doing that. The cops can see what you're doing and all they would have to do is document and bust you. Later I developed methods which I thought were more sophisticated. But in the beginning, I started out with one house, maybe ten people working, and eventually I worked up to two houses. I staked out a neighborhood and I sent my workers out there. You know, I would come to a bar and I would check out a couple of guys and give them from one to five half-a-loads apiece. And based upon their work that would dictate how much more dope, if any, that I would give them.

When I was dealing dope, normally I was in a neighborhood where there were other dope dealers. So we separated our dope at that time by tape—blue tape, red tape, yellow tape—so the people would know who they got the dope from. You know, if you have a bag of yellow tape dope and it was good, you want to go back and get another bag of yellow tape. But you might get it from three or four different dealers, because the same person would have maybe four or five people dealing for him and they would all be selling a yellow tape. You'd be in a neighborhood where there was a lot of competition. So I would get a couple of guys to tout for me, which means I would give each a bag of dope and tell him that for every ten or fifteen customers that he brought me, I'd give him another bag of dope. So essentially, all this touter had to do was to go out there and talk about my dope. I had the best dope. So when customers would come on the block, and the touters would know who's buying dope, they would steer them to where I was, or steer them to one of my dealers.

I'd estimate that for about three months I was pulling in about $30,000 a month gross in my operation. In the beginning I kept records and tallies. It amazed me, I felt like a businessman. Then I started keeping most of it in my head, because the more I got into dealing dope, the more I started to see a lot of hazardous areas, where a lot of people were making a lot of mistakes. At one point, police in New York were busting drug dealers and they were doing it from many different levels. The most common was to make the connection between the street dealer and his supplier—the guy who he's actually picking up the dope from. In the beginning, I used to bring the dope to all my dealers. I would be in the car or I'd drive around the neighborhood and I'd send word to meet me somewhere. They'd bring my money and I'd give them the packages. I used to just walk up the street, and I'd turn around and watch; and then we'd do the transaction right there, but I quickly got out of that. And then it was the cars, and then it was the apartments, and then I stopped doing it altogether. I would send other people out there to do that. I tried to stay as far away as possible from the actual dope itself. But, of course, the more you're away from it, the less control you have over it. I could give one of my runners, let's say, ten half-a-loads and tell him to give it to one guy. Now the runner might take the dope and go home and cut that up. Take that ten and make twenty. Give the dealer ten and he keeps ten, plus the money he's making just from doing the running.

When I first started my operation I got picked up by two detectives in upper Harlem. They knew I was small level at the time. But I had some workers and I was making a lot of money. I think I was making something like five Gs a week. So they busted me. I didn't have any dope or even any money on me, but they arrested me anyway, took me into a hall, and introduced themselves. They told me what the deal was: if I wanted to keep operating, it was going to cost between $1,000 and $1,500 a week. So I struck a deal, started paying them off, and my operation was protected. From that point on, dealing was easier because I could get to know other suppliers and people in the drug culture through these detectives, and I didn't have to worry about getting busted.

My operation lasted about three years and then it ended—a combination of some other police really getting close and my workers, who started to get outrageous. It was hard to control people now; they just wanted to get the dope. You couldn't really trust anybody anymore. It got to the point that in order for me to keep things running, I'd have to do it myself. I couldn't trust them—not with the amount of dope that I was getting. Some of my runners were getting strung out bad. And because they started tapping the bags, what the street pusher eventually ended up with wasn't the same package I sent them. So it was hard for him to make money off dope that wasn't of any substantial quality.

I had to take a baseball bat to a couple of dudes. I had one dude in the hallway one day, not because he took my money, but because he was telling everybody he took my money and he didn't care. It was like he was totally disrespectful of me and that's something that you can't allow in the street when you're dealing dope. You can't have disrespect. So I took him back in the hallway and I took a gun to his head and I pulled the trigger, but I didn't shoot him; it was just by his ear. I took off all his clothes and I beat him with a baseball bat and I left him. And I had two of my workers drag him out in the street naked and bleeding and just leave him in the street as an example.

I remember once going to 127th Street with a baseball bat. I was so pissed off because the guy kept telling one of my runners a story. I would give my runner a certain amount of dope to give to this guy and I would tell the runner that if he doesn't give you a certain amount of money, then only give him a certain amount of dope. I didn't know the guy and my runner was getting soft. The guy was just using him, and I found out about it. And 127th Street and 8th Avenue was not the neighborhood to not have respect in the street. So I drove down and I saw him on the street. He was standing on a stoop, but there was another apartment underneath and when he saw me coming he jumped off the stairs and he was trying to go into that apartment but he was at the entrance of somebody else's house. And he couldn't get away. So I jumped out the car and I began to wail him on the back, and the crowd was growing on the street. I didn't care. I ended up breaking a couple of bones. Then I went and I found his partner. I did the same thing. Once in a while I would have to do that. I remember one Spanish guy that was living in the Bronx. Same thing, it was over money. But in the particular neighborhood that he was in I couldn't allow that. I never really got any pleasure out of it — it was business, nothing personal. These are the things that you have to do. I couldn't send anybody else out there to do it, because it was my respect, not theirs. Eventually, I had a couple of enforcers working for me, but this was near the end, because things were getting so bad and so much out of hand. Things just got out of whack; the dope business just went crazy.

And then there was the police harassment after my operation expanded into different neighborhoods beyond upper Harlem. I was one of the guys that they knew about who was controlling a certain drug neighborhood and they couldn't bust me. They were out to catch me in a transaction and I made sure that they didn't. And that pissed them off, because I wasn't paying them all off either.

I HAD ALL KINDS of customers. I had businessmen, teachers, and police officers. I had correctional officers that used to work at half of the prisons in upstate New York. Everybody gets high. If I were in a white neighborhood, most of the customers were white. In a Spanish neighborhood, heroin is like music: it's a common denominator. White people will come in the black neighborhoods to buy good dope; black people will go into white neighborhoods to buy good dope. I usually liked to deal with the white folks at the time because they had the money and they wouldn't hassle too much. I would usually adulterate the product. I would stretch it. Sometimes I would outright burn them because they would have to come from the lily-white neighborhoods in Riverdale, Jersey, Connecticut, Long Island. They would come right into the middle of the South Bronx to buy a product. And you'd know, number one, they were white; number two, they always had a lot of money; number three, they would come in this nice car. A girl would be sitting in the car while the guy went in to buy, which later on became a telltale sign too. The police would just follow them. Since they had to have dope, they came to where the dope was.

Most of us dealers did a little out-of-town dealing. Matter of fact, I did a lot of out-of-town dealing. I dealt up in Connecticut, in Jersey. I remember one time Lenny, a good buddy of mine, and I had a couple of quarters. A quarter is like a quarter ounce of dope. We'd cut it up into half a quarter and cut those halves into quarters. If you want to take the time to cut it up and bag it, you can make almost a $1,000. So Lenny and I took about fifty twenty-five dollar bags down to Baltimore, since he told me that he knew people down there. I said, "Okay, let's just get a large amount of dope and we'll go down there and we'll sell dope—just make a fast trip, a fast couple of hundred dollars."

Lenny came up with the idea that since he had some cousins in Baltimore we should combine business with pleasure. "Why don't we go down there and hang out in DC and Baltimore for a weekend, but at the same time bring a couple quarters of dope?" So we decided to do this and we ended up going on Pennsylvania Avenue—Dope Street, Baltimore. My idea of what we were going to do was just to be on the street and give out a couple of samples and wait for the people to come back to us. Lenny, somehow, got involved with some people and they were willing to take the sample, but they wanted us to go with them while they shot up the drugs. So we ended up in a basement on Pennsylvania Avenue, and Lenny was busy at the moment grandstanding—taking out a couple of quarters, putting them on the table and putting some dope in the cooker so that the other dope fiends could sample it.

My mind was on the fact that we were in a basement with one entrance and one exit with fifty bags of New York dope. No weapons, because the guns were in the car, and we're in a strange town surrounded by a bunch of strange people who were dope fiends. When this dawned on me—obviously these dope fiends were slow—because had they been New York dope fiends or had the situation been reversed, I'd have stuck them up right then and there, and for all the dope they had, I might have just taken them out. I mean, we had a lot of dope. I'm thinking that maybe they are thinking this, too. But Lenny is busy making friends and is spreading the dope around so that we could make some money, and I had to find a way to sort of pull him from the table and get across to him that we should get out of here right now. And I finally got the idea across to him before these other dope fiends could get organized. Because you see it working in their minds; they were just a little slow. But by the time they had got it together, Lenny and I were already on our way outside of the building. We gave out a couple of samples, and some people bought dope, and we gave them some discounts, because we still weren't losing.

So we're outside on Pennsylvania Avenue and we're selling dope like pancakes, like crazy to customers. We're doing this for about a half an hour and I hear gunshots. I turn around, and I see where the gunshots are coming from, and I also see that they're shooting at us! So I tell Lenny, "Let's get out of here!" We run back to my car, which was parked two blocks away, and I'm ready to get off the block. Lenny is going through this thing about, "Well, yo man, they ain't running me off the block. I'm going back out there and sell some dope."

I said, "Lenny, you're crazy, man."

He said, "No I'm not."

I said, "Fuck it, man." So we went in the car, we got our guns, we came back, and we're shooting back at them.

Well, it wasn't the dope fiends—it was the dope dealers that were shooting at us, because they don't want the competition. We were selling better dope at lower prices. These were the guys who were shooting, which we didn't know at first. So we come back on the block, and we start shooting at them. It was just like cowboys and Indians for awhile and then the shooting died down and we went back on Pennsylvania Avenue. Fifteen minutes after that I hear police sirens. I said, "Oh, shit, Lenny, let's go!" We go back to the car, put the guns and the dope in the trunk and Lenny wants to go back and look around because we didn't finish selling everything we had. I said, "Okay, man, all right." So we got back on the block. We have no dope and we have no guns. The cops come around, they look at us, they search us and they cut out, because we had nothing on us.

Lenny decides that we need a drink and we go into a bar across the street. But down on Pennsylvania Avenue in Baltimore the bars are a little different. They've got a little candy store or something in the front; the bar is in the back. You've got to go through a locked door. So we go through the door and it locks behind us, and it's like a regular bar: drinks, music and stuff. So we're sitting in there and we're having a couple of drinks, and it dawns on me again. I said, "Goddamn!" Here we are inside the bar on Pennsylvania Avenue with no guns, no protection, nothing. I'm starting to see guys come in there that look like violent-type individuals. And I've seen quite a few of them come in the door. And I told Lenny, "Let's get out of here." So first, he says, "No, let's stay, man, they ain't running us out of here." I said, "Lenny, we don't have any guns or anything on us right now." That sort of swayed him. So we decided to have one last drink and we were going to cut out. And it dawned on me again that if they had to push a button to let us in, they might have to push a button to let us out. I was getting depressed. But Lenny had started talking to some people, and then after a while he called me over to where he was talking to this guy. And it was a good thing that Lenny had decided to talk to this dude. Because this is when we found out what was happening. He was one of the bigger dope dealers on the block. And he explained to us that we had come down here and cut into his money and a few of the other dope dealers on the block. It was these guys that were shooting at us. What we should have done was come down there and found out who was dealing dope, sold what we had to them, and we could have made our money and just cut out. But because we came from New York we had taken all of their customers. And they had also just been to New York on a buying spree, so they had dope upstairs that they couldn't sell because we were selling dope. And since they had just bought dope, they weren't in the position to buy dope from us.

They saw that we had heart. And they didn't know whether we had guns on us or not. But we didn't bring it to that type of confrontation. Luckily, the one guy that we did talk to was sort of the major dope dealer down there. He managed to talk to the other dealers and we came to an agreement: we wouldn't sell any more dope on Pennsylvania Avenue at that time. But we did make plans with a bunch of contacts where we would buy dope in New York and we would bring it down to them, or we would meet them half-way, or what have you.

WHEN I FIRST STARTED dealing drugs, I dealt for myself and maybe for the neighborhood junkies. And from that, the more I got into it, the further I got involved in the network. For a while, I was buying my dope from a lot of other guys that had a little money. The bottom level is just a matter of how much money you have. You buy a couple of bundles and you buy a couple of half-a-loads, and you sell it for a small profit or just to support your habit, which a lot of guys did. They would take maybe thirty dollars and buy half-a-load, sell half, and they would use the other half, but then they wouldn't have to spend any money. The next level up is when some-one will have just a little more money. At this point, none of this is really organized, you know, as far as any type of crime organization. There's just really not that much money involved. Dope fiends, at times, will accumulate a lot of money, but they're not very particular about where they spend it except on drugs. So sometimes they would have the money. And everybody who uses drugs ends up dealing at one point or another on that small level one way or another. Once you score and get more than enough money to support your immediate habit, you would buy for tomorrow. The wake-up shot is always on your mind, so you can at least have a shot to get you going during the daytime. If you scored big and you got enough money, you'd buy a half-a-load, maybe two halves. And because you have it, you're going to let peo-ple know that you got it. Or people will find out that you have it, and you'd sell a bag or two.

The higher-up dope dealers are always looking for low-level drug addicts or low-level drug dealers. You really didn't have to go looking around for someone to let you deal, like you were putting in an application for a job. People would approach you to sell their product. They see how you han-dle yourself; they see how you handle their product. And they already know that you're going to use a certain amount of the product. But they're willing to buy into the lie just as much as you're willing to spread the lie that you can handle it, you can take care of it. You know, I'll sell X amount of drugs for you, and I'll keep X amount for myself, and we'll keep the money right here. Which is all bullshit, because there are very, very few people that I know who both sold and used drugs and kept their money straight. Your habit will always come first. And if you've got dope, you'll use it—I don't care whose dope it is. You could have a bundle of dope from a big-time organized crime boss, and if your habit said you needed to get high, you would shoot that dope and think about dealing with him later.

Usually, the connections came to you. What we saw from dealing on the street level is that sometimes we knew a pusher who had dope, and if the dope was good, he usually sold out. And if he didn't have enough drugs right there, he would have to call the person who supplied him. And that person was the next level up. And this guy would come to one or two of his pushers and he would bring a couple of bundles of dope. And everybody would be waiting, because if the guy sold out with the good dope, he would get word by telephone, messenger, or somehow to his connection that he needed some more dope. So he would then wait for his connection to come down, and they would go somewhere and exchange money for dope, because you would have to give up the money from the dope you already sold before the guy will give you another package. And sometimes, he knew that you had messed up his money, but he was willing to give you some more drugs to make it up on the next package—which is another lie. Because sometimes you do it and sometimes you don't. But by the time dope gets down to the street level where you're selling two dollar bags, five dollar bags, you could take a big loss financially if you bought a big chunk of dope and you cut it up—I mean dope as opposed to street cocaine, which you could cut only three times at the max, and then it's garbage. I've seen heroin that you can cut maybe sixteen times, so you're working on a sixteen hundred percent profit and you can afford to take that loss.

I always knew who my suppliers were at the next two levels up, because these two people would have to meet at one point or another; or I would know either by word of mouth, the grapevine, or some other way. The higher up you went, the more these people tried to stay incognito. But I think something that's inherent with the dope world is flamboyance. It's difficult not to flash what you're doing. In the beginning, like in the sixties when I got involved, there was a lot of flashiness. After police crackdowns, arrests, and a lot of violence, people started to tone that down a little bit. But it's hard, because you have to conceal a great deal of money. The people that were selling dope made a large amount of money because a lot of people bought dope. And it's hard to conceal that, especially from a dope fiend.

In the beginning the Italians had the dope. They controlled it. If you wanted a big chunk—let's say if you got an ounce of "pure dope," which is the kind of skag you could cut sixteen to twenty times—you had to get it from an Italian. Blacks and Hispanics just did not have those connections at the time. As a low-level dealer at that point, I never saw the transaction being made. But I knew from other people where the dope came from. And I knew who controlled what was coming in. But I couldn't put my finger on them, and I couldn't approach these people by myself. The Italian Mafia guys were mainly in the financing and distribution. I didn't go to any Italian guys to get dope; I had to go through an intermediary. But the Italians kept a very big distance between themselves and the low level or the black and Hispanic dealers. In order for you to deal dope for them you had to go through three or four different channels. Eventually, the Italians got to dealing with some of the big black dope distributors, like Danny Jones [a fictitious name], you see, but this was after a while.

I knew I was getting dope from one of Danny Jones' lieutenants. I dealt directly with him for a while and I used to get a lot of dope from him. I got to talk to him, and he knew I was buying. He was a co-partner of Danny Jones. He didn't buy dope from Danny. They all got down when there was a buy. And this guy had money—he kicked in his money in the pack. It's like a hierarchy: Danny was the king, and a couple of other guys were like lieutenants, because they were still directly under Danny. They were in charge of enforcing, distribution, and everything else. And in doing so they had their own pieces of dope, so they also had their own networks. But the dope came from Danny. He was the funnel it all came through.

EVERY ELECTION YEAR, DOPE WOULD dry up. It would get tight, because the politicians would make sure that the dope wouldn't come in. They wanted to get those votes from the people in the neighborhoods. This is the time when most people got busted, because we had to go outside of our normal supply groups to Jersey, Connecticut, different parts of the city. And most of the time we had to take a chance on the dope and you couldn't buy a lot of it. Whoever had it would make money by just giving up a little bit here, a little bit there. They would only give you so much for a certain price, and then you figure if you're buying wholesale — if you're buying a lot — you've got to get a discount. But it wasn't like that. Sometimes you could only buy dope that was already packaged — scrambled dope — that was already for street distribution. Most of the time when you started dealing dope, you wanted dope that you could cut. Why buy some dope that all you had to do was package and set out there when it cuts into your profit margin? But if you can buy an ounce or a half an ounce of dope and cut it up ten or twelve times, this is where your profit comes in.

WHEN I WAS SELLING DOPE I would use people because I knew that they had to have dope. So I would make them do what I didn't feel like doing. I would send them out to rob, to steal; give them ideas about where to go and what to do. Give them a little bit of dope and send them out there. Bring me back this, bring me back that, do this, do that, and I'll give you some dope.

"Give me some dope now."

"No, man, I'm not giving you anything, not till you bring that back." It changed me, I didn't think I was that mean. But it's business. It's one of the dirtiest businesses that you can get into. And as long as you treat it that way you'll maintain some kind of profit.

Sometimes I wouldn't have any drugs, but I'd still have

my habit. Since I had a reputation for selling drugs, people who didn't know I was out or people that were just coming into the drug scene would still come to me to buy drugs. What I would do is I would sell them a dummy, which is anything from baking soda to Alka Seltzer in a bag. And they wouldn't open the bag or check it out in front of me; they would buy it and then walk away. And I'd disappear. Or the people would come to me and I'd take their money and I'd tell them, "Well, wait right here, I'm going to my stash, I'll be right back." But I wouldn't come right back; I'd be gone. Or I would go to people that I knew had drugs and would tell them I had a lot of money; I want to buy a lot of drugs. And they would produce the drugs and I would produce a gun and I would take the drugs. There was a lot of that going on. Because every once in a while there's a panic or the police would make a lot of arrests, and drugs in certain neighborhoods would dry up. And it was not just myself; I mean, there was a lot of people that were doing these things, ripping other people off. And it got to a point where people bought drugs and they would open a bag in front of you. So this way you couldn't tell them, "Well, you didn't buy that from me," or "You took the bag and you walked away and you switched bags." I used to do that too. I would buy good dope from somebody and then walk around the corner and come right back and say, "Yo man, this is garbage. Now give me my money back." You know, I was switching bags.

I'VE NOT ONLY SOLD drugs, but I've also provided protection for other drug dealers. I remember one incident when I was about twenty-eight, a few years after my own drug operation had ended. Alvin was a stickup partner of mine that knew this guy named Julio, who was a big dope dealer in Manhattan. And he was out of business for a while, you know, and then he decided to go back in the business and decided he needed protection. Alvin needed a partner, so Alvin got me. Alvin and I used to go to Teaneck, New Jersey and pick up the dope and go down to Manhattan to some of the cutting houses. We would go with Julio when he picked up his men and his workers. We had a couple of altercations where Alvin and I had to go and rough up some of Julio's workers. Alvin shot a guy one time. We had gone to the building; the guy was inside and Alvin had wanted to take care of this himself, so he just told me to wait outside. I knew in the back of my mind that Alvin was going to do anything from blow the guy's head off to cripple him. I didn't see, I was inside, but Alvin did shoot him in the leg. Again, I didn't really feel anything, it was business; it wasn't anything personal. I didn't really care one way or the other. My job was protection, to see that nobody took anything from Julio. And I was paid well for it, so that's all I did. Everything else I just ignored. And Julio used to make sure that we had dope.

5

C H A P T E R

THE NUMBERS GAME

As an active junkie, you're always thinking about money. I myself never liked to gamble, shoot dice, play cards or numbers and all of that. I always thought it was a waste of time. I always like to play the sure shot. When I was about 30 years old, I lived in a three building complex, and we used to have a uniformed doorman downstairs to keep out the riffraff of the South Bronx. George, the doorman, used to take numbers part-time for people in my building. One day, I had some money and I went and bought some dope, and I was spreading a little bit of it around. So I figured, "Oh, what the hell, let me take a chance on these numbers here." So I gave him a couple of dollars and a number. I think I hit that day. I always have this phenomenal luck. Whenever I do something for the first time, I win a little bit of money. But for some stupid reason I always thought that gambling was addictive, so I never wanted to get into gambling. I used to see old ladies bet every day—nickels, dimes, pennies. They bring it down to the numbers man—you know, it was a dream. And I didn't want to bet my life on a dream. I couldn't see that as a dope fiend I was doing worse than they were. But I used to know George, I used to talk to him a lot, and I had made something like thirty-five dollars on a five dollar single-action number bet.

George told me I would have to wait for Manny at the end of the day to pick up my money.

When Manny came by he was cool. He was a Spanish guy from across town. He had a Cadillac and a flamboyant style. After he paid off the money for the other runners, I met him and we got to talking a little bit. A couple of weeks after that Manny would come by every day. He asked me to start running numbers for him, because he was trying to recruit people to go around the neighborhood. He was a controller and the more people that he had working as numbers runners the more money he was taking in. I resisted the idea for a while because I didn't think I could make enough money to support my dope habit and I sort of liked doing the other things that I was doing. And I didn't have the time just to hang around the neighborhood all day long to maybe make X amount of dollars. I just couldn't see any money in it. But I was married at the time, and I was living with my wife. She sort of pushed me to get involved since it was the lesser of two evils. She'd rather have me doing the numbers, which is considered a clean crime, as opposed to being out there shooting and robbing and stealing. So I told Manny I'd do it. He gave me a pad and a pencil and some of the other customers in the building. He started to spread the word around the neighborhood to come to me to bet your numbers, because I was one of Manny's men. I was a numbers runner. Early in the morning I would go to people's apartments in my building, and they would give me their bets. They would bet anywhere from a quarter to a dollar on a three-digit number. Mr. Bateman and some other people, they'd bet big: five dollars on a big digit number or a combination of three digits.

Many of my customers would buy dream books and every time they had a dream they would look up the number in the book. I mean, the numbers business was crazy. People would walk by something with a number, or they would look on your shirt—a certain color—and they would get numbers from different colors. They would ask what your birthday was or what floor you lived on. The numbers game is like a subculture. Certain numbers would be heavily played: 769. Christ is seven—I'm not sure why—and sixty-nine has a sexual connotation. People used to like 721. A lot of customers liked to play triples. There are certain holidays like Thanksgiving, where 024, 204, 240, you know, some variation on November 24 is played. The same thing with New Year's and Christmas. The day that the space shuttle blew up, the time. I mean, all of that stuff was played. Events that happened. Like Martin Luther King—when he got killed. When Kennedy got killed. People just grabbed numbers out of the air.

My regular customers played every day. Sometimes they would give me money and numbers on Monday, and just play straight through the week. They'd give me seven dollars for a three-digit number that they played every day. And I'd see them next week. I mean this went on every single day. I had my regulars and then I had other people that would take a chance every once in a while.

One of my customers was an old lady, and I used to hate to go there because she would play three-digit numbers for nickels and dimes. But nickels and dimes add up. I would go to her apartment and she would have them all written down on a piece of paper, and I would have to write them down on my number sheet. And I used to get tired of that since I would waste maybe a half an hour in her house for a dollar fifty. So it got to the point where I brought over a carbon paper, and I said, "Listen, when you write your numbers out at night, you write them on the carbon paper, because I'm not going to spend all this time in here counting these goddamn nickels and dimes and writing down all these five cent numbers." In the morning, I'd go around and I'd pick up my numbers from my local customers. And then I'd go down and either hang out in front of the building or hang out in the grocery store. I'd walk around the block. Being a numbers runner kept you stuck to the neighborhood, because people had to find you.

The way it worked, I made money. Most of the time for a five hundred dollar hit—a three-digit straight hit—I'd make $150 from the controller. I'd get maybe a twenty-five or fifty dollar tip from the person that hit. If the hit was too big, Manny would call me and let me know how he was going to pay it off. And I would in turn tell the customer. Either

Manny would give it to me, or he'd have it at the spot; and I'd take the customer and drive him or her there, or I'd tell the customer to get your son or I'd get somebody to go and pick it up.

THOSE GODDAMN ITALIANS CONTROLLED the numbers racket. You got independent numbers bankers, but they all have to deal with the number that comes out. I mean, the Italians have control over that. The guys at the racetrack are the ones that control that number. If there's too much play on a number, they'll change the number. Basically, people would find out the number the day after from the last three digits of the "handle" (the total gross receipts) at a certain track, figures which were printed in the *Daily News*. Let me tell you about how they change the numbers sometimes. I had to wait for Manny to call me to let me know what number came out. At the end of the day you get your three-digit number. Since I was a numbers runner, I had to report to the controller. The controller reported to the banker, who was the person financing the numbers operation. The bankers, of course, reported to the organized people—the Italians—who were in control of the numbers. If there's too much money being wagered on one number, and if this number comes out, we would go broke. So what the bankers did was lay off the numbers to other bankers. In other words, if I kept bringing in more money based on the same number, then my particular banker would stop taking the bet and he would send that bet over to another banker who is willing to take the chance that the number won't come out. When that happens too much, and the bankers start laying off, or they find that too much money is being wagered on that one number, there's a high possibility that number might be changed. When Manny calls me and tells me the first number is seven then I go pay off my single action customers. If that number has changed and I'm out in the street away from any telephone, Manny will come and tell me to stop paying off on that seven—they changed the number.

Numbers and loan sharks go hand in hand, because we have cash money—unreported money. I would walk around sometimes with two thousand or three thousand dollars in my pocket. If I wanted to take a chance and loan somebody four hundred or five hundred bucks based on their word, I'd take some gold or some property from them. If I could cover that with Manny without him finding out—or tell him and get his okay to do that—I'd do it. For a loan of five dollars I want seven dollars back very shortly—within a week at the most. If I could get away with more interest, I'd charge more. I would only lend out small amounts of money. But I know Manny and some other people lent out money to other people.

A couple of times Manny made some mistakes. I remember the first big mistake he made. The number was 571 and I had turned in the money bet. Manny told me that there were five hits for that number that particular day. But I only had recorded four hits on my sheet. I don't know how he got five hits on that sheet. So I got $650 because it was a five-to-one payoff. And I couldn't remember or find out who that other hit went to, so I kept the money. I don't know how he screwed that up over there, but the bankers gave in and Manny never found out. Sometimes I'd play some of my own numbers. I'd pay for them and I'd turn it in. But I would also supplement my income by dipping into Manny's money to pay for the dope.

If the business would have kept up, it would have been very lucrative. But we were having a lot of problems too, because there were numbers joints opening up in the late seventies. So the day of the runner was like the day of the gunfighter; it was becoming a thing of the past. Because people could go through a little hole in the wall around the corner—a numbers parlor, which is like a little office with a plexiglass window, and you come in there to play your numbers. And that's what put the runners out of business. In the numbers joints, people are wishing and dreaming. They stay there, and some people pray. Some people just hang out drinking beer, and just walk around anxious, hoping that their number will come up. And they want to be right there, the second that number comes up, because they want to pick up their money right away. There are a lot of number joints and they are still illegal. But as long as you're not doing it blatantly, the cops usually overlook that, because numbers is considered a clean vice. It probably still is. There's usually no violence and drugs and things like that involved.

PEOPLE PLAY NUMBERS BECAUSE it's tax-free money. When they started the lottery, basically what the state did was have people continue to play in two different places. If you hit six hundred dollars on the lottery, you have to fill out the tax form. You've got to pay taxes on that money. The reason that illegal numbers was started was to make tax-free money. It's part of the ghetto culture. Anyway, if you can make some tax-free money you're going to do it. The state tried to tell people that the lottery is safer, your money is guaranteed, because people started having problems. Hitting the illegal number is one thing; collecting your money is another. So many independent numbers operators started to sprout up; and when they started to get hit too much, they just wouldn't pay the people off. And the person you really had to deal with was basically the numbers runner and maybe the controller, if the customers knew who the controller was. But the banker and everybody above him didn't have to worry about that. I know people that have hit five thousand or ten thousand dollars and were shot dead trying to collect their money. You know, the banker would pay off and they'd go to the numbers runner to collect, but somewhere along the line either the controller or the numbers runner would keep the money. It's just like any merchant: you have to know who you're selling your goods to, and feel comfortable that you can collect your money. There was a period of a couple of months where there was a lot of violence involved in that. People were taking in armed escorts to go pick up their money. Then you can't find the banker. If you're honest and pay off your customers then your expenses go up, because you've got to get protection. All the other people — the criminals, the dope fiends and everybody else — know somebody hit big, and they would wait. They would lie in wait for these people to pick up their money. Or some of the less honest numbers people would inform other people of the customers they're paying off these large amounts. And they would give the people their money, and let the people go home or get away from the premises, and then the people would get ripped off.

I worked as a numbers runner for about seven months. I started to dip into the money; and at the same time, Manny was having problems with some of his workers, problems keeping the money straight and paying off. So he eventually got out of it and so did I.

WE USED TO STICK UP numbers joints because, again, that's where the money was. They were like store fronts, like a liquor store. You can go in, go up to the counter, play your number, and get a receipt for your money. Before they started using plexiglass and different things in the back, they used to do this over the counter. So a lot of times we would go in at the spur of the moment — just walk right in. They used to keep all the money in a box, right there behind the counter. And we would go in and sometimes push the guy away, or maybe hit him in the head with a pistol, back him up, reach over and snatch the thing and run out.

The biggest score I ever made from a single robbery in my life was $105,000 when I stuck up a numbers bank in 1977. Since I used to be a numbers runner and because I was a pretty trustworthy guy, at that point, I met a lot of people. I met controllers and I met bankers in the numbers game. And these are people who have the money, who fund these numbers operations. And I also found out the Mafia or the Italians didn't control all of it. The numbers game was for whoever had the money and the muscle to protect their operation. So I chose two Spanish guys to rob that I knew had the money and I checked them out for a while. I even followed them home one night and drove to their house in Yonkers to see where they lived. At first it was just a thought in my head. It was maybe six months between that first thought and the actual robbery. Up until the time that it happened I never really planned on doing it. It was just that I was meeting all these people and I knew where all this money was. I even told two other guys about it, what to do, where to go — everything. At this particular time I didn't have any money. I had been out of the numbers game for about two months now because of my dope habit. I just wasn't reliable anymore. And people that I used to collect money from knew that. My banker and my numbers controller knew that too. So they didn't like to put money in my hand. I was desperate for money because I didn't have any, and I would've stuck up a kid down the block or a dope dealer or something in order to get money. So I decided to rob these numbers bankers. They were small freelance operators, Dominican guys who came over to New York and had a lot of money. They were into a lot of dope; they had a couple of numbers spots in Brooklyn as well as in the Bronx; they were into stolen goods, and they had a couple of grocery stores in Manhattan and Brooklyn. They had money.

I drove up to their neighborhood. I had a pistol in the car, because I had taken it when I left the house and put it in the glove compartment. I had a little bit of dope left so I drove off the highway and I got some water and I shot the drugs in the car. Not enough to really get high but enough to get me straight, to take the edges off. The plan was coming together in my head as I was driving up to the joint. So I drove around the neighborhood, passed the house, and parked. I'm about seven blocks away and for some stupid reason I'm hoping that something would happen and I wouldn't have to go through with this. I was alone and I really didn't have anybody pushing me, saying, "You have to do this." So I parked the car and it was about 7:00 or 8:00 in the evening. It wasn't quite dark yet, but it was getting dark. And it was in September so it wasn't that cold. I was dressed for the neighborhood, so I sort of fit in, but not really. You know, blacks in a white neighborhood. But I had a brand new car, a Buick Century Regal. Brown, not flashy—it wasn't a pimp's car—but it was kind of classy. It was nice. I used to buy a car every year. I ran through a lot of money. At the time I could get a brand new car for like six thousand, seven thousand dollars cash. I had a car dealer on Boston Road who never questioned me about where the money came from and I gave him a couple hundred on the side just to keep him quiet. It was nothing illegal—I mean, I paid for the car, the papers were legit, but you had to fill out IRS forms and everything else.

So I parked the car and I started walking. My mind still wasn't set yet on what I was going to do. I got up to the house and then I looked around and started to knock on the door.

I was about to walk in the front door, and I'm starting to think, "Well, who's home? I wonder if these guys got guns? Are they going to give up the money easy? You know, their wives are there; their kids are there." And as I was starting to think about all this stuff, my body is walking around to the back of the house. They have a pool in the back, so I walk through the gate, which happened to be open, and I remember thinking, "Well, once I walk past this gate, I've got to do it."

I walked past the gate and then there was no more hesitation—I just walked in. It was kind of amazing. The back patio door was open. They were upstairs on the second floor; I guess it was like an office that they used. I put on a little ski mask, a black one with two eye holes and the mouth thing, and I had leather gloves on. I took out the gun and I walked in. I heard them typing on adding machines. So I went upstairs and I pulled the gun and told them it was a stickup. There were two of them. And the younger of the brothers said, "Just don't hurt me, just don't hurt me." I said, "Get away from that table. Get over by the window and lay down flat." So both of them went over there. I looked on the table and I was figuring there was somewhere around $20,000. It seems like they were holding out on people, because they had more money than they were supposed to have. But this is something I found out later on. There was like maybe $20,000 on the table wrapped up in rubber bands with little slips in there on how much is in each package. They had a safe on the right side of the desk and it was open. And that's where I found the rest of the money. It was over $100,000. I didn't panic; the size of the money didn't change what I was doing in any way. It was just numbers at that point. And they really didn't offer that much resistance. I was covering them with the gun and with the other hand taking the money out.

It seems like I was in there maybe an hour or so just stacking money. And then I started worrying about the fact that there's so much money here—small bills, big bills—and what the hell am I going to put it in? Anyway, I ended up taking a duffel bag out of the closet. I filled up half the duffel bag with money, and I looked for something to tie them up with. I found some clothesline rope, cut that up and tied them up face down on the floor. I had some tape and I taped it to their mouth. I was worried they might get hurt. The old guy, who was in his fifties, might have a heart attack. I tied the rope from their hands to their legs so I had them sort of in a U-shape, kind of bent backwards.

I didn't think about it at the time, but afterwards as I was driving home I thought, "There's nobody else in the house!" The kids weren't there; neither one of their families was there. No protection, nothing—just them. Later on I found out through the grapevine that the youngest guy's wife came home about forty-five minutes after I left. I never told anybody else about this robbery because that could get you in a lot of trouble. People get mad about getting stuck up.

After I took the money, I got in touch with this fine broad I knew and told her I had a lot of money and drugs and let's party. Before she got to the hotel I had gone and purchased a couple of bags of dope, some cocaine, and some champagne. I had all this in the room by the time she got there. But before she arrived, I dumped all the money on the bed and it filled up the bed; it was a king-size bed and I jumped up and down on it for a little while. You know, all this dough, all this money. Then I started counting it, which presented a problem, because I had a bed full of money. Ones, fives, tens, twenties, fifties and hundreds. There weren't too many big bills and I ended up having stacks of ones, stacks of fives, stacks of tens, stacks of twenties. This is numbers money, which usually comes in small bills. I still had a small shopping bag, maybe half of it filled with money. I had no idea how much was in there. But the money I had gotten was like $105,000 in round figures. I had rubber bands and numbers slips and dollar bills all over the room. By the time the girl got there I had gone off into my fantasies. Laying up with a girl in a bed full of money, drinking champagne, shooting dope and thinking about buying anything I wanted to buy. With that kind of money I figured I could buy the world. But that dream lasted for about two months and three weeks and I was broke. I had bought a Corvette, flown to California, bought clothes, and I gave money away, which didn't present too much of a problem because people in the neighborhood sort of knew me as a person that always had money.

To my knowledge, the numbers bankers I robbed never found out who did it. I think if they did I would be dead now. They had a contract out on a person, unknown, who did this stickup. I felt a little heat once in a while but since they really didn't have direct proof, I just walked around like it wasn't me.

6

SLIPPING THROUGH THE SYSTEM

NEW YORK CITY HAD AN OPER-
ation authorized by the city police to infiltrate drug neighborhoods and make mass drug-related arrests. It was called
Operation Pressure Point, because it targeted the most drug-
infested areas. I got caught up in it one time in 1987. I was
on Avenue D and 8th Street in Lower Manhattan, and I
bought two bags of dope, but I didn't have a set of works.
I went upstairs to my friend Jerry's house. Jerry had a set
of works and he was going to get high, but I didn't want to
wait for him—I wanted my own works. They kept warning
me that Pressure Point is downstairs, that the cops are watching and you're liable to get caught. So stupid-ass me, I go
back downstairs, right back in the middle of the dope, and
I bought a set of works. I was walking out of the block when
some guys started yelling in Spanish across the street, "Watch
out, the cop is behind you." And by the time I turned around,
there was a blue uniformed cop, and he collared me: threw
me up on the wall, put a gun on me and found the works.

The cop put me in a van that was parked around the
corner, and when they got enough guys in the van they took
us downtown. When I got inside the van, the cops already
had sets of works wrapped up in little bags. And not everybody that they caught had dope or works on them. The cops

thought it was a joke—they said, "Okay, what did you get him with?"

"Well, he was buying some dope from the guy, but he must have eaten it or something."

The other cop says, "Well, fuck it, this set of works is his—here." By the time we got to court, everybody was charged with something, whether they had something on them or not. And so I ended up going to the Manhattan County Jail—the Tombs—for two days.

Usually when they catch you with a set of works or something minor they give you a desk appearance ticket. But because it was part of Operation Pressure Point, you had to go to court to a judge. There was no bail; there was no desk appearance ticket. You had to wait to go to court. What they were doing was watching and busting dope dealers, dope buyers, people with works. The object was to disrupt the drug traffic, because the police were putting the pressure on the drug points all around the city.

As far as making a dent in the drug traffic, it didn't make a bit of difference. As soon as the cops move on, the neighborhood returns to normal, or if Pressure Point stays a while, the dope moves to some other location. Some of the people that were caught up in the Pressure Point net had outstanding warrants for other charges. So they were filtering out a few of those people, but they were also arresting other people who were just part-time drug users, people that were working who just liked to get high once in a while. Very few hard-core addicts were caught up in that operation. The hardcore addicts managed to slip through it anyway.

Even with the record that I had—I was still on parole from an earlier bust—by the time I got to court, the legal aid lawyer told me to cop out to loitering, and I would get time served and walk out of court, so that's what I did. He said, "Are you worried about a conviction with your sheet?"

I said, "Hell, no."

He said, "Well, I'll tell you what. The DA is willing to accept the plea to loitering. You cop out to loitering and I'll get you out of here right now." And that's what happened.

I HAD SPENT THE NIGHT at a friend's house. This was a couple of days after the Pressure Point bust. I called up a girlfriend in Albany to send me some money to get out of New York, and she had sent me one hundred dollars by Western Union. But I was sick from the drug withdrawal, and I got together with one of Jerry's friends. I was going to take him by the methadone program, and he was going to get some of his methadone so I could take some of the sickness off before I went to pick up the money. But then Jerry's mother gave me ten dollars. So I went downstairs and I bought a bag of dope and I was going to shoot that. And as I was driving to the corner on the way out of the block, I saw the cops and I knew that they were going to stop me. I put the bag of dope in my mouth and I think the cop saw me do it, because he didn't search me or anything when he stopped the car. He just pulled me over and asked me what I was doing in the neighborhood. And he knew that I didn't have a driver's license. So he asked the guy next to me if he had a license, and the guy said, "Yeah." But it was bullshit, and the cop checked in the computer and found that he didn't have a valid license either. But I guess it was just something that they didn't want to deal with, even though he saw me swallow the dope. He told me to get the hell out of the neighborhood and don't come back until I have a license.

There was another time I had to swallow dope to avoid arrest. I had gone to New York City from Albany. I didn't have a car or anything, and I went down to New York by bus to buy some drugs and bring it back up to Albany. And everybody warned me against doing it, but I had a hard head. So I went to New York, bought two bundles of dope, some cocaine, and some reefer, and I got high on the bus. But when we pulled into Albany, things had gotten so hot that the police had set up a little station right there in the bus terminal. As I got off the bus, something told me to put the dope in my mouth. All I had to wrap it in was cigarette cellophane, but I had so much dope that it was hard to put it all in there. I had dope and cocaine in there and a five dollar bag of reefer. So as I was stepping off the bus, I put it in my mouth. As I turned around to walk into the bus terminal, a cop grabbed me on the back of my neck and he turned me around. He started asking me where I was coming from and what I had in my pocket. I had all of this shit in my throat so I couldn't talk. I'm telling him, almost whispering, "My name is . . . I just came from New York, from the Bronx."

He said, "What's the matter with you? Can't you talk?"

I said, "Yeah, man, my throat hurts."

He said, "That's bullshit," and he started to put his finger in my mouth, and that's when I had to swallow it. It was so much it wouldn't go down right away. And he kept sticking his finger in my throat, trying to grab it, but what he was doing was pushing it further down.

I ended up swallowing something like fifteen bags because I had bought two bundles, which is twenty bags. I did five on the way up, so there were fifteen individually wrapped bags, plus some cocaine and a nickel bag of reefer. He's got me up on the wall now by my neck. They're asking for my ID, so I show them ID and I'm kind of scared, because I was still on probation at the time. And I have to report these contacts to my probation officer, so I'm worried about this, and I'm worried about all this shit I just swallowed. The cop told me, "Look man, I know you swallowed it, but I'm not going to bother taking you in. But I do suggest that you go to Albany Medical Hospital and get your stomach pumped out." There were a lot of guys bringing back cocaine from New York City, and the cop probably figured what I swallowed was like an eighth or a couple of quarters of cocaine; and he knew that you can kill yourself if that stuff bursts in your stomach. He didn't know that I had swallowed heroin. The cop says, "I ain't going down your throat and pull that shit out, but what I suggest you do, man, is go on up to Albany Medical Hospital and tell them you swallowed some shit, and don't kill yourself. Go on up there and take care of it."

But I didn't go to Albany Med. I went to another hospital. I was sitting there, and I told the broad that I had swallowed some pills, and that I wanted to bring it up. But actually, in my dope fiend frame of mind, I was so pissed because I had swallowed all this dope; and I was trying to get it up so I could salvage some of it to shoot it. I tried to dig it out on the way to the hospital, but I couldn't get down far enough. I went to Bobby's house first — this guy I used to know in Albany who used to play in a Latin band with us — and I told him the story. People had given me the money — it wasn't mine — to go to New

York to get drugs for them. And I ended up swallowing it. And I wanted to tell these people what was going on. In the meantime, I'm sitting in this house and I'm starting to feel the effect of some of the dope, because some of those bags burst. And I'm saying, "Goddamn, that's two bundles of dope I got in my system—I'll go out." I started nodding all over Bobby's bed. He said, "Man, you better get to the hospital."

So I went to the hospital. I get there and they give me some stuff that makes all the shit come up. But what came up was soggy and everything; I couldn't salvage anything. I knew I had to finally tell someone in the hospital what was happening. So when the nurse started to give me medicine to throw up, she started figuring out what was happening. I said, "Listen, if I tell you something, you can't call the cops on me, right?" And she knew where I was leading, so she said, "No, I wouldn't tell the police. What did you swallow?" And I told her, "Two bundles of dope, some cocaine, and some reefer." Then she said, "I'm glad you told me because the medicine that I was going to give you would have been the wrong stuff and you would have gotten sick." I thought, "Two bundles of high quality dope—I would have probably overdosed."

The people that I owed the money to were pissed off at first, because they figured it's just another dope fiend game. "He's telling us this bullshit because he blew the money." But some other people happened to see what happened to me that day and told other people. A couple of days later the story got around. People said, "Yo man, you all right? We saw the police grab you off the bus."

The police wanted a bust, but they didn't feel like taking me to the hospital with all those drugs in me, so I slipped through the system again.

ONE TIME I WAS REALLY doing bad in the city. I was living in the Bowery, because I had some dope dealers looking for me. I had the cops looking for me, I had three outstanding warrants, and it wasn't safe for me in my old haunts. I was stealing batteries out of cars to support my habit and living in this stinking-ass hotel for Bowery bums. So one day I decided to burglarize this place in the Bronx. I went up and I burglarized it. I got some cash money and I stole a TV. The day before, I had something like one hundred dollars, so I got a hotel room at the Lexington Hotel downtown on 53rd Street, and there was no TV in the room. At the time I had two sets of works, about five caps of coke, and about six half-a-loads of dope on me, plus the stolen TV. When I go into the hotel with the TV, I'm not paying any attention, because I'm trying to go upstairs to my room to get high and watch television.

I was dressed like a dope fiend, and this is a middle-class hotel. I come marching in the goddamn hotel with this little portable TV under my arm, and as I'm getting on the elevator these three cops walk in. The guy shows me a badge and says, "Yo man, is this your TV?"

I say, "It's my TV, why?"

"You sure it's not hot?"

"No, it's not stolen."

"Where do you live?"

"Up in the Bronx, but I'm staying down here." In the meantime, we get to the seventh floor and we walk into my room. I didn't have to let them in the room, but when we got to the room, I'm just giving him straight-up answers, you know. Meantime, I've got all this dope, all these works. So we get to my door and I open it. The cop says, "Do you mind if we come in, because we want to check out the TV?"

It was only three o'clock in the afternoon, and in order for the TV to be on the hot sheet, these people would have had to come home from work. It would be at least six or seven o'clock at night before this TV went on the hot sheet, if it did go on the hot sheet at all. I said, "Yeah, you can check it out"—you know, to stop them from searching me or the room or anything else. So me and the three cops are in the room. At first, one cop calls up whoever he calls to get this type of information. He describes the television and everything else, and he's stealing glances at me. And I'm playing it cool now, because I know the TV is not going to be hot. But at the same time, the other two cops are starting to get restless, and they're starting to look around the room. I say, "What you looking for? This is my room; you haven't got any warrants—you can't be looking around here." And then I eased off of that because it doesn't matter if they have a warrant or not. And I didn't want to start playing smartass, because all they had to do was search me.

They're opening drawers and there's nothing there. I had another stash from yesterday, which was in one of the top dresser drawers in the back. Now I'm trying to figure out how not to panic or keep looking at that drawer. In the meantime, the cop is waiting for the information on the TV, and the other two guys are just starting to get more into the search of the two rooms. So I asked him if I could go to the bathroom, and he looked at me and said, "Sure." I still had my coat on, so I'm standing in the bathroom—he let me go to the bathroom by myself—and I threw all the dope and everything that I had in my pocket in the toilet. I pissed, flushed the toilet, and came outside. I'm out of the bathroom now and I'm standing there now, you know, I'm cool. At the same time that they tell one cop over the phone that the TV is not hot, his partner found my other stash. He found the works and the other dope that I had in the drawer. So they bust me for robbery, possession of works, possession of narcotics. We get downtown and all the other warrants drop. I thought, "Oh shit! I'm looking at one hundred years on all these charges." So I talk to legal aid, and legal aid is telling me, "You can forget about going home. You're going to have to go to the Bronx, to Queens, and to Brooklyn on all the other warrants." I had gotten busted several times before and walked out of the court, either on bail or on my own recognizance, and I never went back.

So I'm sitting in the bull pen and I'm waiting. And one of the cops that busted me comes in, a Spanish cop named Rodriquez, and says, "You know, you've got all these other cases and everything out there. What are you going to do? You got a family?"

"No, it's me and my mother."

He says, "Look man, you seem like a nice guy. I've got a way out for you."

I said, "What are you talking about?"

He says, "If you're willing to work with the narcotics unit, I can get all of this shit taken care of."

I said, "What do I have to do?"

He says, "I'll let them talk to you. But if you're willing,

we'll keep you for seventy-two hours, which is the law. We can't get you out before that, because you have all these warrants on this other stuff. You stay in here for seventy-two hours and you walk out of here; those warrants will be dropped; the charges that you got busted on will be dismissed. You'll walk out of here, and I'll send these two guys to talk to you from the special narcotics unit."

I said, "Fuck it, what have I got to lose?" So I laid in the Tombs—the County Jail—for three days. I went back to court, and I walked out of there. Welfare got me a sleazebag hotel in the Bowery. So I'm sitting in the room and these two bulls come in. They were in suits and carried attaché cases. One guy was black, one white. They come into my room and we're sitting down talking. The first thing that dawns on me is that I'm in a dope fiend hotel. These are narco cops. Everybody that lives in the building will know that two narcos came here and are leaving without me, which brands me a rat off the top. So I'm thinking about this. In the meantime, these guys were all business.

One guy sits down and opens up his attaché case. He's got a couple of guns in there and some pads of paper and stuff. So he takes it out and tells me the deal. He says, "Listen, this is what we want you to do. You know what a John Doe warrant is?" I said, "No."

He says, "A John Doe warrant is when we get a guy selling dope directly to the police. We know his real first and last name. He makes a sale to an undercover cop and we don't bust him right away; we bust him maybe five or six months later, so that the suspicion doesn't fall back on you. What you have to do first of all is you've got to know the legal first and last name of these pushers. You have to take an undercover cop with you to make the purchase. The undercover cop has to make the buy. You just introduce them. You keep the money, and you keep the dope. And here's a telephone number. If you get busted for anything up to and including homicide, you call this number and you'll be out of jail in an hour." He says to give them a couple of weeks to set it up, and they'll be in touch with me. They left me some money and then they split.

I sat and I thought about it. Number one, there weren't

too many guys that I knew by their first and last names. I knew Flacko, Tito, Fat Bob, and Julio, but I don't know these guys' real first and last names. The second thing is, I'm just not that type of person; I'm not a rat. And it would be real hard for me to live with myself like that, because at first I would think, "I'm mad at every dope dealer that never gave me a break—I'm going to rat them all out." But I turned that over, and I couldn't do it. I'm playing the scenario over in my head and saying, "Wait a minute, I've got to take an under-cover cop with me to buy dope." How am I going to do that in a dope fiend neighborhood? An undercover cop sticks out, especially a white undercover cop in a black or Hispanic neighborhood. They're going to know, even if they do bust them five or six months later, which I've seen happen. I've seen guys sell dope and then clean up and get out of the trade—legitimate jobs and everything—and police snatch him with a John Doe warrant.

"What the fuck you talking about, 'John Doe'?"

"Well, we got you for selling dope."

"I ain't sold dope in six or seven months. What are you talking about?" That's when he sold dope to an undercover agent. And the warrant is legit, because the cop is the one saying that he sold dope to him—and he did—and the cop testifies. So I thought about it, and I just couldn't do it. I couldn't live like a rat. It's just not in me. None of this street macho criminal code shit—I mean, me as an individual, Ron Santiago. I could not do that.

I thought it over for two days and I went to see that cop Rodriquez back at the precinct. And I sat down and told him I couldn't do it; and that I wasn't going to run, so whatever you're going to do, do now. He looked at me, and he saw that I was serious, so he said, "Listen, I'll tell you what, if you go into a drug program, I'll still keep everything squashed. But if you leave that program, I'm coming back down on you with everything." He says, "Clean up your shit, man, you seem like a nice guy. Go to a program and clean up and get out of this." And I did.

I think we've got some good cops. And, I don't know, I guess he saw some things in me that I didn't see myself and he was willing to give me a break. I went into ARC—Addicts

Rehabilitation Center. This was the second time I had gone through this particular program. And I knew that James Allen, the director, had a center in Jersey. Since I still would have had the cops looking for me, and I still had other people looking for me, I told Allen I want to go to the joint in Jersey. He says, "Where are you?" I said, "In the downtown 20th precinct." He said, "I'll have a car there in an hour to take you straight out to Jersey." I stayed in the ARC for about twelve months. I stayed clean for a couple of years after that.

THE SYSTEM DOESN'T WORK. THERE'S no such thing as justice. It's about how much money you've got, what color you are, what particular crimes you got busted for, who you know, how much weight you got, how much juice you can pull. That's what the whole thing is all about. There were numerous guys that I got busted with, and I would watch them walk out of the court; guys busted with tremendous amounts of narcotics walking right out of court at arraignment. Drugs in their pockets at the precinct or in the property bag, and somehow, the drugs would disappear. I know a couple of guys that used to work with cops. They used to brag about it; they used to tell me about it. You know, "I'm not worried about being busted." Or, "This fucking guy busted me, man, he must not know who I'm working for." When you were buying drugs in the street, it was common knowledge who the supplier to this particular dealer was: the guy was a goddamn cop!

From the judges on down to the prosecutors and assistant DAs—I'd say all of them could be reached. I've seen some crazy shit happen in courts. I've seen some guys walk from two murder charges. Robberies broken down to breaking and entering and being told behind the scenes what had happened. You know, money. Even if they had a videotape of somebody pulling the trigger on somebody and the body being right there—I mean, irrefutable evidence—I've seen guys walk from that. I knew that they were involved in the crime and I knew that they and their family had a lot of money and a lot of connections. And that's what got them out of there.

Before you even get to court, when you get interviewed

in the bull pen, the lawyer is more or less telling you what's going to happen, because he's already spoken to the DA, and he already knows who the judge is, so he's going to tell you what to say this particular time. If he thinks this judge is kind of rough on this particular type of crime he'll tell you, "Do this at this time, and then we'll get it taken out of this judge's court into another judge's court." And, "I think this judge is a little more lenient towards what's going on, where I can get a better deal." Or he'll tell me, "The DA that's up there is pretty shitty but the judge is all right, so we have to take a shot." So this is the way we played it.

By the time you get to court, unless you get a new legal aid, you're just another name in the game they're playing. And the circumstances of your case is the only thing that gives variety to what they're doing. Legal aids are training to be private lawyers or DAs. If you get a legal aid who's training to be a DA, I suggest you switch lawyers. From the time you get arrested, you know, from the precinct to central booking to arraignment, you're there with other convicts, other inmates, other guys that have been busted. Rarely will you be in there with somebody who's been busted for the first time and who doesn't know anything about the system. Obviously you get to talking about your case because you're worried. Somebody will hear details of your case and they'll tell you, "Well, listen, man, you tell your lawyer to do this." Or you can do this, or you can do that. So by the time you get to talk to a legal aid, you've already got a few ideas in your head about what's going on.

And if you don't like what the legal aid is saying, you could always waste the court's time by telling the judge you don't like the lawyer that you have, and you want another one. Or you could insist on a jury trial—that's part of the game. "If you don't give me what I want, man, I'm going to take it to trial." It's a hassle; it'll never go to trial. Whether it's a big offense, a petty offense, or what, they don't want to go to trial. But if you take the chance and push it all the way to trial, and you lose, they'll stick it to you. But you learn. Not everything you learn inside the bull pen and before you get to talk to your legal aid is going to be valid, because a lot of times the legal aid is going to tell you that's bullshit, and you can't do this and you can't do that. "I don't know who told you this, but it's wrong and this is really what's happening." But if you got through the system a couple of times, you get to know which legal aid is on the money. I had a guy who first told me to cop out. And I told him, "Fuck you, I'm not copping out to anything; and if this is all that you're doing, you go tell that judge when I go up there right now that I want you off my case. And I want time. I want a postponement to get another lawyer." That's my right to be represented by counsel. And if I think that my assigned counsel does not have my best interest at heart, then I can demand another legal aid.

If you're doing really well and making a lot of money dealing dope, eventually, you'll hire your own private lawyer. I had a lawyer—Nick Felino. Nick had connections with the DAs and judges in the Bronx Supreme Court. If you had a dope case, go to Nick. It would cost you, but Nick would let you walk. Private lawyers always get more respect in court than legal aid lawyers. Once in a while, you find a sharp legal aid who's in it because he cares. I've been fortunate, I've had a couple of these. I've also had a couple of shitheads—I fired them. Most of the time I didn't have money, so I depended on the public defender or legal aid. But I still chose who I wanted to represent me. In one case I went through maybe four lawyers until I got one I wanted. The judge was getting tired of postponements, and the DA wanted to take it to trial, so I had to play part of the game too. "Yeah, we'll set a trial date," I said. All I was playing for was time. So we set a trial date for a couple of months; it was still getting me time to get the lawyer that I wanted to get the best deal.

I HAD JOINED THE NAVY at age nineteen in 1966 to get away from the dope. I didn't really think that I had a problem with it; I just knew that things were getting kind of difficult. I knew if I kept up in the street dope world, I'd eventually end up in prison. But when I joined the Navy they wanted me to be a boatswain's mate or a radio man, which I didn't want. I had taken classification exams and I had qualified to go to school for electronic's technician, but they bullshitted me, saying that training schools were closed. If I wanted to learn a trade, the only one I could learn was to be a boatswain's mate. I didn't want to do that so I ended up on a destroyer for a couple of months and I got sick of that. They had me with a torpedo man from Texas. I mean, he was a good guy and the crew and everything was okay, but I just couldn't see staying on the destroyer and not learning anything. So I put in for a change of orders. I decided if they weren't going to let me go to school for electronics then I was going to put in for a Navy aviation assignment. My thinking was that I would get an assignment to a land base in Texas or Florida and lay up for four years and just hang out and party.

Because I had put in orders for transfer they had taken me off duty on the tin can and sent me to the Brooklyn Navy Yard Transit Barracks to await my other orders. When I got to Brooklyn, they had initiated a new work detail: you work for two days and then you're off for two days, so I had two days to hang out. Since I lived in New York, I would go home for two days. One of my drug connections used to live right across the hall from me. So I joined the Navy to get away from dope and they put me right back in the middle of it. I would go home, get high, and pick up my package, so when I came back down to the Navy I'd always have a lot of dope. I started selling dope to anybody and everybody. And word got around the Navy Yard: if you want to buy dope, go to the boiler room and ask for Ron.

Eventually, the Office of Naval Intelligence got involved. I was in the boiler room, which was my work assignment, and one day this white guy came down who I had never even seen before, but that didn't matter, because I sold dope to everybody. He bought four bags of dope and he left. Maybe ninety seconds later, Arnie, a Spanish guy and one of the cooks, ran downstairs and asked me if I had sold dope to a white guy. And he described him, told me that the guy was working for the Office of Naval Intelligence, and that he was a cop. I said, "Ah, to hell with it." You know, partly, I didn't believe it, and partly I didn't care. I went behind the boilers in the back, shot two more bags of dope, and ended up going back upstairs to my quarters. About fifteen minutes later, the Master at Arms came in with this lieutenant who had bought the dope from me and told me that I was under arrest for selling dope. I was high at the time and I said, "Fuck you, I'm not under arrest, I'm not selling any dope, and I'm not going anywhere."

I guess they never had anybody as belligerent as I was at that point, because they didn't know what to do. They kept telling me to get up, I was under arrest, and I said, "Fuck you, I'm not getting up, I'm not doing anything, I'm staying right here." So they left, which was amazing. What I should have done at this point was leave. But I was so high I just lay down. The Master at Arms came back with some bolt cutters and some marine chasers—guards. They broke open my locker and they took the rest of my stash. I had some pills, some reefer, a lot of dope, and my money. They forcibly took me off the bed and took me upstairs to the brig.

I began to sober up a little bit and it started to dawn on me that they were serious about locking me up. They had me upstairs and they were taking off all my clothes. This one marine, Sergeant Jackson, who was a little shorter than me—the little motherfucker—he liked what he was doing, making me take off my clothes and barking all these orders. We didn't click at all, so Jackson said something to me and I looked at him and I said, "Fuck you, man, you do it." Jackson grabbed me by my T-shirt and he threw me up on the wall. Instantaneously, as my head bounced off the wall, my hand came up and I knocked him out. The brig warden just happened to be standing over there, and he saw what was happening so he ordered all his guards to get me.

They kicked my ass and threw me in what they call the cell block. It's like concrete walls with a cell door and armed guards standing outside. There's a light that stays on all the time. They would open the cell door a little bit and they'd kick in the box lunch. So I started going off in there, because the dope started to wear off, and I began to realize where I was and what was happening. They had taken me out to fingerprint me and I went off again. I started banging on the marines, and the marines jumped on me again and started kicking my ass. But all the other black and Hispanic inmates in the brig had gone to the warden and told him, "Get the marines off of Santiago, because if you don't we'll turn this brig out right now." And in a military brig, in this one anyway, the inmates have razors and all that other shit that they got from the barbershop and places like that. And when they went and told the warden that they were going to riot if they didn't get the marines off me, that's what the warden did.

He threw me back in the cell block for a couple of hours. Then they bring this young white guy in who was AWOL and they lock him in the cell next to me. He starts screaming, "Mommy! Mommy! Help! Help! Let me out. I can't take the confinement." So half an hour later they come and open the cell, take him out, and send him to the hospital. I thought, "The hell with this." And I started yelling, "Yo Mommy, help! Get me out of here! Get me out of here!" The riot squad came. They said, "If you don't shut the fuck up, we're going to beat you to death in here." I said, "All right, that's cool, that's cool." So half an hour later an ambulance did come, and they took me out of my cell. They put me in a straitjacket and tied me down to this stretcher.

In the meantime, I hadn't had a cigarette in about a day and a half. So I'm asking one of the marine guards to give me a cigarette and this guy's looking at me. For some reason, you're supposed to go along with this treatment and everything else they tell you to do. The fact that I was belligerent and didn't give a shit and had no respect for them at all was unusual. So I had to intimidate the guard—chasers they call them—into giving me a cigarette, lighting it, and holding it so I could smoke it. And to this day I don't know how I could have scared this kid. Here I am strapped and tied down, can't do anything, but I said, "Man, I'll kick your little ass; give me a goddamn cigarette." He got nervous and gave me a cigarette.

I didn't know it at the time, but they were taking me to St. Albans psycho ward for two reasons, which I found out later. The first was that the longer I stayed in the Third Naval District brig in Brooklyn, the more likely I was to cause a riot. Because everybody up there at one time or another bought dope from me, and they didn't appreciate what the warden was doing there. And they knew what was happening. They really wanted to protect me, because I used to do favors for them too. You know, that's another part of the subculture of dope.

So anyway, they sent me to St. Albans psycho ward. I get over there and the first thing they do is put me in a lock-in ward. There's no walking out of that ward. You had to get medication four times a day, because at that time unacceptable social behavior was treated with drugs: thorazine, librium, morphine and chlorohydrate. But this is where they started screwing up. I'm in St. Albans psycho ward and I wake up; I get my medication and my body is slow, my mind is slow; I can't do anything. I stay there for about three weeks. And one of the guys who was in there had his family visit him quite often, and his sister took a liking to me. She used to see me through the bars, and she told him to tell me that there were no confinement papers on me in the office and that legally, technically, they had no reason to hold me there.

As soon as I found that out, I went up and yelled through the bars, "Yo man, let me out of this joint. I want to go home!" They were laughing and I said, "Get me a doctor up here right now and check that board. You don't have any confinement papers on me. You have no legal reasons to hold me here — get me the hell out of here." The smile left the guard's face and he went and got a doctor. The doctor came back upstairs and he looked on the board and he checked everywhere else, but there were no confinement papers on me. They didn't have any orders; they were holding me illegally. But they couldn't just let me go. So what they did is they transferred me. I was in D-2 psycho, which is a lock-in, and they transferred me to C-2 psycho, where you could walk around the hospital but you had to check in with the Master at Arms every four hours.

And this is when I started to find out a couple of things. After the naval intelligence agent bought the dope from me, he left the Brooklyn Naval Yard because Arnie and the rest of them had threatened him. They were going to kill him if he stayed there. So he left a signed statement and they reassigned him somewhere else. I spoke to some lawyers, and I found out that transferring me from the Third Naval District brig to the psycho ward was illegal. The warden did it because he didn't want me to cause a riot in his prison and also because he thought I was crazy. That was the second reason they took me to the psycho ward. And they had arranged all this just by phone calls. There was nothing legal or legitimate about this. But they had never had a major narcotics bust up until that time. They had AWOL, fighting in a bar, maybe catching a guy with some drugs on him, or something else.

By this time, I'm starting to figure out where I'm at and what's going on. So I started having a little fun, because I found out that when you got that armband on that says "C-2 psycho," you're not responsible for your actions. You can do anything you want to do and they can't do anything to you. This is about the time I started causing trouble throughout the hospital. I would go in the barbershop and I would throw stuff around. There would be other military personnel coming in there—captains, colonels, sergeants—getting haircuts, and I would curse them out. I would make them get out of the chair. One time this Lieutenant Colonel comes in and he's waiting for a haircut, and he gets ready to get in the barber chair. So I spit on him, pushed him out of the chair, jumped in the chair, and told the dude to cut my hair. The Lieutenant Colonel is going crazy. "Who are you sailor? What's your name and rank? You wait right here." He calls the Master at Arms and thinks he's going to get me locked up and sent away to some prison. So I'm laughing at him. When the Master at Arms comes, he listens to the complaint and then the Lieutenant Colonel tells him who the guy is, and they look at me, and the Master at Arms says, "Oh, you mean Santiago." He tells him, "Well sir, there's nothing you can do about it; he's a patient here in C-2 psycho. There's nothing you can do about it." Oh man, he got pissed. He got super pissed. So I spit on him again. I left and went to the chow hall. I started throwing shit up in the air, trays and everything. I left there and I went to the movie theater. They never physically assaulted me or anything. I guess they figured I really was crazy. But it was a role I was playing.

Three weeks after I was put in C-2 psycho, three lawyers came to see me. They were all Navy lieutenants; one had just come out of Vietnam, one was just coming in the service, and one was just getting out and going into private practice. And they sat down and they told me what the deal was and that I was going to beat this case. I was charged with seven counts of selling narcotics. I went to my first pretrial hearing and they scheduled me for a general court-martial. I was facing forty-nine years, my lawyers told me. They were going to work together since they wanted to take this case for the legal experience. And they told me that I was going to beat it, but I had to jump through a few hoops first. So they sent me up to Portsmouth Federal Penitentiary for a couple of months.

The lawyers told me they usually get these bullshit cases: fighting in the bar, minor narcotics, AWOL, or something like that. They all wanted this different kind of legal experience. And I gave them that experience. They told me what I would have to do. "You have to chill out. They're going to send you to Portsmouth, but don't worry about it; we're going to get you out of there." So I went through Red Line Brig, a military jail. Red Line Brig is like a state penitentiary, except there's a red line going down the middle of the whole brig; it's like a yellow line down the middle of the highway. Traffic moves on one side of the line and the other side of the line. But it's a little stricter because they'll bust your ass quick.

So I stayed there for a couple of months. One of the naval lawyers came up to visit me and said, "How'd you like to walk out of here?"

I said, "I would like that very much."

He says, "I'll tell you what, I'm going to get you out of here today. But I can't get you out on the street. This is what's going to happen: we're going to send you back to Brooklyn Navy Yard for a while." And what he meant was that I'd have to deal with Evans, the Judge Advocate over there.

But Evans was a geek, man. He's a chump. He's always trying to make his legal case. You always thought he was a legal eagle and he ain't shit. Evans says something and everybody jumps, everybody's scared. So I knew I'd have to deal with him, and that he can get real, real petty, which he did. My first day back, I wasn't locked up or anything. I was just back in Brooklyn Navy Yard. No security confinement, nothing. They assigned me to barracks back upstairs again and I went to the gym. In the service, they have staircases designated "Up," and staircases designated "Down." Evans busted me for running up the down staircase and gave me fifteen days restriction for that.

While I was on restriction, I was the only one in re-stricted barracks that had his ID card. You're not really locked up, but you're restricted to where you can go and do things. And they take your ID card. But I still had my ID card the first day I was on restriction and I was in charge of giv-ing out work assignments. I had it easy. I was just sitting in the paint locker; and when it came time to give out work assignments in the morning, I would hand out the paint brushes, brooms, and mops, and then I would go downstairs. I'd go right in front of the Brooklyn Navy Yard, take a bus to Skillman Street, which is about fourteen blocks away, buy some dope, come back to the Navy Yard, and go back upstairs to the restricted barracks. And I had a partner, and he and I used to sit up there and get high all day long. Evans knew I wasn't supposed to have an ID. He also knew I wasn't sup-posed to be walking around by myself, because once you're restricted, you eat and work together as a unit.

Evans was scared of me by then, because here I am fac-ing a major narcotics arrest. And here I am back in Brook-lyn Navy Yard, not on restriction or anything else, and still awaiting orders for my aircraft carrier or my base in Florida. So Evans didn't know what legal power I had. And he was scared of the juice that I had.

During the fifteen days that I serve on restriction, my lawyers are researching my case and I'm really not yet under indictment in the service. They've got me scheduled for a general court-martial. Because of the weight of the charges, everybody messed up with the paperwork. Everybody. I was on an aircraft carrier on my way back to Nam when they found out where I was physically located. I did my fifteen days on restriction and my orders came in. I even had two days liberty before I had to go pick up my aircraft carrier in Norfolk, Virginia. And I was pissed off because I wanted to go to Florida and hang out. So they got me on an aircraft carrier and I'm out at sea for four months. Finally, some orders come through, and marine chasers come to my sleep-ing area. "Santiago, we got to take you back to Brooklyn under armed escort." I said, "For what, man?" I thought they had forgot all about it. I did. But I had to go back to face my general court-martial. They didn't know where the hell

I was. And I wasn't running, man. They sent me orders, I picked up my orders, and I reported to my ship.

So they fly me back on one of those little A-4s. We get back to Brooklyn and they lock me up. I had seven pretrial hearings and during my second one, we're sitting there and they offer me a cop-out: twenty-one years! If I cop out to twenty-one years, they won't give me the forty-nine when they finally find me guilty at the end of all these hearings. I told them, "Listen, anything over one year is too much for me, man. I'm nineteen years old; you're talking about copping out to twenty-one? I'm not copping out to anything." And my lawyers told me, "Don't cop out to anything." The naval DA comes over and tells me the deal and so I laugh at him: "Get the fuck out of here. I'm not pleading guilty to anything."

In the meantime, my lawyers are telling me how they're tearing all of these charges down. Motions here and motions there. All kinds of illegal procedures. The fact that the naval intelligence agent will not testify in person. They got his signed statement thrown out. The arrest was illegal. Sending me over to psycho ward was illegal. Busting into my locker taking all the drugs—all this evidence was illegal.

I go to my seventh and last pretrial hearing. My lawyers are there. And every time I went somewhere—every place I walked—I had handcuffs and shackles and a red armband and two marine guards because I was considered a dangerous person. So I'm standing there and I'm looking at my lawyers and they're avoiding looking at me. And this seventh pretrial hearing wasn't a scheduled one. They just came up to my cell one day and said, "We've got orders to take you to court, let's go." I'm standing there and my lawyers are just laughing at each other and talking to other court personnel. They aren't paying any attention to me. This is the first time I started to get scared. I thought, "Wait a minute; they sold me out. I'm going to have to do forty-nine years!" I was so scared that I started shaking and my chains were rattling; that's how scared I was.

Then they start these legal proceedings, and nobody has said anything to me. The judge is starting to talk—and I didn't plead guilty, you know—and he is starting to read off my charges. What's going on? So I'm looking at my lawyers and they're still not looking at me. A lot of things ran through my mind. Then the judge starts reading all this legal shit and he says, "Charge one." It seems like it took twenty years for him to say the next words: "Dismissed, evidence insufficient to sustain a conviction. Charge two, dismissed, evidence insufficient to sustain a conviction. Charge three, dismissed" and so on down the line. Then my lawyers looked at me. I said, "You motherfuckers!" They did it, they did it—they got me dismissed! And I turned to the guards and said, "Yo man, take this shit off me, I'm a free man; take all this iron off me."

I was in the Navy about three years. I got an honorable discharge. In fact, the day I got my discharge, they offered me two thousand dollars plus my choice of duty stations if I would re-enlist. I told that broad to give me that piece of paper and let me get the hell out of there.

I'VE HAD A LOT OF close calls and managed to slip through the system a number of times. I remember when I was living in Albany in 1988, and I had gotten kind of lazy because I had really started to get strung out on dope again after I got out of prison. I was forty-one, and I didn't really want to get involved in robbing and things like that to support my habit; so I had to settle on just going back and forth to New York, because you can buy dope there for ten dollars and sell it in Albany for thirty dollars. That had become quite lucrative as far as I was concerned. In my stupid way of thinking, it was the lesser of all the other evils. So I had taken to driving back and forth to Brooklyn and the Bronx, buying bundles of dope, bringing it back to Albany and selling it.

On one particular trip, I took Maria, the wife of a friend of mine, down to Brooklyn because I used to buy dope in her mother's neighborhood. So we went down early that morning and stayed all day in her mother's house. I had already gotten busted on the New York Thruway for drug trafficking. And I was dealing with a court case in Woodbury, New York, for transporting narcotics, which I was currently on probation for. But even that didn't deter me from going back and forth to New York. So Maria and I got to Brooklyn early and I bought a couple of bundles of dope, some cocaine and some reefer. And we stayed at her mother's house until late that evening getting high and bullshitting. So we decided to leave to come back up to Albany. We gas up in Brooklyn, get on the Brooklyn-Queens Expressway and start heading out. By the time we got to the George Washington Bridge I had two choices: I could have gone straight up the New York Thruway or I could have gone through Jersey. I didn't have enough gas, so I decided to go through Jersey because the gas was cheaper. And this was a split-second decision. I didn't even know which way I was going to take.

We cross the George Washington Bridge and we hit Route 4 and I pull into the Getty station. And while I'm gassing up, a guy gets out of his car, walks over, and asks Maria something. And when I finished pumping the gas I went back in the car and asked her what that was all about. And she told me the guy was asking directions. And for some reason, something clicked in my head. I said, "That's bullshit, that's the police!" So I got back in the car and we started driving off a little further on Route 4. I keep looking in the rearview mirror, and there are two detective cars right behind me. At this point, there's not much that I can do. I could have probably turned off at any point, but I thought, "What the hell, I'll bluff it out." So when we get to the turnoff from Route 4 to 17 north, there's a right turn off of the highway. And as I turned on my right turn signal and began to make the turn, police cars came from everywhere. I'm hearing sirens, lights; there are cars behind me, cars in front of me, cars on the side of me. They had me blocked off, so I had to pull off right there.

As I pull over to stop, all these cops are coming around the car—there are shotguns, guns everywhere. "Stop!" "Don't move!" "Freeze!" Maria's so hysterical and high that she's reaching into the back seat in the grocery bag for something—she had done some shopping while in Brooklyn. I don't know what the hell she's reaching for. I'm saying, "Maria, don't touch those bags." And the cop stuck the gun at her head and said, "Don't move! Leave them bags alone."

I was high. But as normally happens when I get into critical situations like this, my high starts to go down a little bit and my intellect starts to take over. I'm trying to think real quick. With all the dope that I had on me I knew that if they found it I was going away for a very long, long time. So at that point, I made a decision: If they found the dope, I was going to run. And if I ran, I knew that they were going to shoot me. But I had decided that dying was a better alternative than spending the next twenty years in prison.

So the cop is sticking the gun at Maria's head, telling her not to move, and to get out of the car. And there's a guy on my side of the car and he's talking to me. But he's real cool about it. He puts his gun away, since there are guns everywhere, and there's not much we could do. So he starts this shit, "Let me see your license and registration for the car," and "Where are you going and where are you coming from?" So I tell him I was coming from Brooklyn; I had my friend and I took her to Brooklyn to go shopping for groceries. In the meantime, she's arguing with the other cop. She wants to get something out of the bag and the cop is trying to explain to her that there could be weapons in there, and he wants me to tell Maria to stop reaching in the bags. Maria at this point is speaking in Spanish. She can speak English very well, but she's speaking Spanish and the guy's asking me to interpret—to tell her to chill the fuck out, because the other cops will blow her head off if she keeps reaching for the bags. So I told him there's nothing but groceries in there; if they want, they can check out the bags.

In the meantime, this guy's talking to me and they got Maria out of the car and they're checking out the bags, and he sees nothing but groceries in there. This guy's real cool, though; he's not sweating, nothing. I tell him, "Here's the registration and everything for the car, but I don't have any license. My license is suspended." He says, "All right, do you mind if we search the car?" I said, "No." So he gets me out of the car, and he tells me to empty my pockets, which I did except the pocket where I had the drugs. It was in the wintertime, so I had on a T-shirt, a sweatshirt, and one of those pullover hood sweatshirts with the pockets right in the front and another jacket over that. All the dope was in the right hand pocket inside the pullover sweatshirt. And on my way stepping out of the car, I just sort of mashed it, so that it didn't bulge real big. We get to the back of the car and my hands are on top of the trunk and my legs are spread out. All these cops and guns are everywhere again—guns in my ass, in my ears, in my head. On the other side of the car they're talking to Maria. And Maria's raising hell in Spanish with them. They're searching the car. There's nothing in the car so I'm not worried about that. I'm just worried about what I have on me. This cop is still making small talk to me, but at the same time he's searching me. He'd stick his hand in my back pocket, find nothing in there, and he'd step back and he'd look me in the eye, like he's trying to read me.

Actually, there was no probable cause for them to stop me. But I felt at the time that I wasn't in the position to argue with them about my legal rights. Plus it was the DEA—the Drug Enforcement Agency—the Jersey State Troopers and one New York State Trooper. There were about eleven cars all together. I was trying to figure out why they stopped me, but I had to put that in the back of my mind for now. What I had to deal with right now was this cop finding all this dope in my pocket. So he's looking at me while he's searching me, and he's playing a little game. He didn't just search all of my pockets at the same time and throw me on the car. He's talking to me, because I guess in the back of his head—you know, since they didn't immediately find anything in the car and he didn't immediately see anything—I guess he was toying with this legal rights thing also. He didn't want to blatantly just go through a complete body search with me, so he did it subtly. All my stuff, my wallet, my money, my keys are on the trunk of the car. While he's talking to me—again small talk—he's sticking his hand in my other pocket searching me: there's nothing there. And we're talking some more, and then he sticks his hand in my front left pocket in my pants. There's nothing in there. At the same time he's talking with me, he's looking at me, like trying to intimidate me, or read me— read my response—and I kept having this urge to put my right elbow over the pocket with the drugs in it. But I knew if I did something like that he would immediately go there. So I was playing a game, trying not to give off signals to him that I was scared or that I had something somewhere for him to go ahead and check.

We're standing there playing this game for a while, and I'm looking him dead in his eye. And every time he'd ask me a question, I'd answer it. I don't take my eyes away from him. I don't do any other body language or anything. He and I are locked into this game now. But for some reason, I feel that he's toying with me, that he knows that I have the dope and he knows exactly where it is, because all during this search he's sticking his hand in every pocket except the pocket with the dope. He reaches into the left hand pocket in the hood sweatshirt—it was one of those sweatshirts where it doesn't go through; it's like two separate pockets. I thought, "Man, it's only a matter of time now." I started to kind of lose faith and I was just getting ready to run. And during that time I said a silent prayer. "God, if you get me out of this, I'll leave dope alone from now on." Getting me out of this seemed to be an impossible task, because they had caught me red-handed, dead to rights. Obviously they had followed me, and obviously they knew who I was, and obviously they knew what I had. But I guess it was just something I felt like doing at the time, praying to God to get me out of this impossible situation, which I knew wasn't going to happen. I knew God would have to work overtime to get me out of this: no license, living in Albany, coming from Brooklyn, all this dope. I had a current narcotics transportation case in the courts right then, I was an ex-parolee, and I would be sentenced as a predicate—a second offender—felon. I mean, there's just no way out of it.

Maria is sitting in the front passenger seat of the car. First they took her out to search the car and then they searched her a little bit, as much as they legally could since there was no female officer there. But when Maria had left the gas station, she had stashed all of her drugs and works in her drawers. And this is in the winter time and she has a lot of clothes on. I didn't see it as being necessary to stash my dope. It was going to be hard for me to do it anyway, because the detective cars were behind me and they would have seen me lean down or something like that and I think it would have been a dead giveaway, so I had decided to bluff it out.

We're at the back of the car and this guy's looking in my face. He's talking and putting his hand everywhere. And there's a pocket right above the dope in the leather jacket

I have on. And he stuck his hand in there, but for some reason I guess his hand tilted out as he was trying to feel if there was anything in it. The pocket was empty. Then he stepped back, and he looked at me and he started talking to me again. Then he'd look at me and he'd reach over and he'd stick his hand in my other inside leather jacket pocket, and he's still looking at me, still talking. And he backs up. "You ever been arrested?" he asked.

"Nope."

"Do you use drugs?"

"Nope." And he goes into my back pocket again. By this time maybe twenty-five minutes have gone by. As they don't find anything on Maria or in the car or on me, they're kind of frustrated; and some of the cars are starting to leave, because it's starting to look like they screwed up or they can't find the drugs. So now it's down to about three cars. There are two DEA cars left and one Jersey Trooper car. The guy is still talking to me—still doing this shit—he even looks in the little watch pocket that I have on my dungarees. Every time he comes near that pocket where I have the dope I've got to keep some kind of self-control not to give myself away.

By now, it's starting to really dawn on me that something's not right. Either he knows that the dope is there, or during this bullshit search in my pockets he forgot which pocket he looked in and which pocket he didn't. He was also getting half-assed frustrated. Because he can't break me down; he can't intimidate me with his little game that he and I both knew we're playing. So he's starting to talk to the other officers. "You find anything?"

"No, there's nothing there." They tore up the front and back of the car, but they could have looked in the engine. They could have looked in the trunk, but they didn't. So he's still standing there talking to me, and he's starting to go back in pockets that he's already searched. He never searched down my legs, down my back. He never body searched me—never. I mean, I could have had the drugs in my shoe. I could have had them in my drawers. So I think he was hoping I'd make a dash for it, and then they'd have some legal pretext to shoot me.

By stopping me, by searching me, and not finding anything initially, I think they were legally constrained in what they could do further. I think he was trying to go about it in a slow half-assed way—giving me time to do something—knowing full well there's nothing but police all around there. If I run, I'm getting shot. And I know it, because I wouldn't have stopped; they'd have had to kill me. So I played his game right up to the end. I wasn't going to give myself away; he was going to have to bust me. The three times when he reached over in the right part of my body—like when he went into my leather jacket—I just took my arm up and I gave him room. When he looked in my right dungaree pocket, I leaned over and I gave him room. We were playing this mind game and this eye contact game. But I guess in the end he didn't know I had that dope. He had overplayed his hand.

There are still a few cops standing there, looking directly at me, guns right there. And they were trying to prompt me into doing something. They really didn't search the car too much, just the immediate area—the bags, the glove compartment, and the stuff right there. You know, because should they get to court, they want to say, "Well, he ran and that gave us probable cause to search. Well, he did this, which gave us probable cause." I wasn't giving them probable cause to do anything. I stood there and I cooperated. And I knew that they didn't have the right to do that.

We're standing in back of the car and he's still going through my pockets, and the wind blows. Like I said, I had all my money, my wallet, my keys and everything on the trunk of the car. So the wind blew away some dollar bills I had on the car. I began to reach for them and then I stopped, because I started hearing all those clicks: the cocks go back on the hammers of the guns. And I remembered. So I stopped. I watched my money blow and I said, "Is it all right if I go pick up my money?" He looked at me one last time, and he said, "Yeah, go ahead." I went over and I picked up my money, but I put it back on the trunk of the car. I didn't put anything in my pocket. I didn't want him to be back in my pockets for anything. I put the money back on the hood of the car and I put my wallet on top of the paper money. And I stood there.

So he played this for another fifteen or twenty seconds, looking at me, and he said, "Put your stuff back in your pocket." I put my wallet back in my left pocket, I put my money and my keys in my right pocket and he stopped me. He reached in my back right hand pocket again. Then when he took his hand out, he said, "All right, get the rest of your stuff and sit in the front seat of your car. Sit behind the driver's wheel. If what you told me about your license is true, we're not going to give you a ticket, but I just want to check and make sure all the information you gave me is correct." I tried hard not to laugh at that point and I got behind the wheel of my car. At that point, the state trooper left, so there were only the two DEA agents. I already knew what was going to come through the computer—I didn't lie to them— my license is suspended and the car is registered, insured, inspected, so there's nothing wrong with the car. There are no warrants on the car. I had a current court case, but I didn't have any warrants on me. And my court case was in New York, not New Jersey.

I'm sitting in the car and a couple of minutes later the guy comes back and returns my registration, my insurance card, and says, "Sorry for the bother. Get your license straight." I said, "Yes, sir." And I got the hell out of Jersey, laughing my ass off all the way back to Albany—scared to death. I couldn't figure out why this guy didn't body search me, and why he didn't find the dope. And I knew that they had to know who I was. Shortly after this time they started a task force in Albany. They were stopping cars on the Thruway coming from New York with drugs in them. They were stopping guys getting off the bus in downtown Albany with drugs from New York. So I think they knew my car and they knew who I was because I was selling dope in Albany. I mean, it's a small town. Or maybe someone ratted on me.

7

C H A P T E R

GOING TO JAIL

THE FIRST TIME I GOT arrested — I think I was sixteen years old — they called me a youthful offender. I had gotten drunk and wandered into a firehouse; they charged me with attempted robbery and breaking and entering, although I was eventually acquitted. But that was the first time I had been arrested and taken to a precinct and sent to jail. It was the Manhattan County Jail and it was nicknamed the Tombs.

I was scared to death, because at sixteen I had heard a lot of stories about jail. I guess, up to that point, I had assumed I would never be in jail. So the threat of jail really didn't make a dent in my head or my character or anything. It didn't stop me from doing anything; I just automatically assumed that I would never be in jail. So I was quite frightened when the cops came and took me to the 35th precinct on 135th Street between 7th and Lenox Avenues, which is one of the most notorious precincts in Manhattan. They had us in there — there were three of us involved — and they took us to this detective in the squad room. They were also bringing in some other people that they had arrested. This is when I really started to get scared, because in a precinct there's nothing but cops. And they're all around, and they're doing different things, and they're all laughing. It seems like the cops always know that those of us that they are arresting are going to go through a lot of changes, while they're going to go home after their shift, so they don't really worry about what goes on.

The cop who had us in there was taking all this clerical information, but in the meantime he had locked us in a holding pen, which is about ten by sixteen feet. So you're locked in there with a bunch of other people who have just gotten arrested for different crimes. People that have been through the process before were just more or less chilling out in the bull pen, and we were panicking like crazy, trying to pretend that we were hard criminals at that point, and we weren't. I was taking in everything at this time. The precinct has like a certain smell to it. There's a lot of sweat, there's a lot of fear—fear's thick—you can smell it. And there's a lot of lying; there's a lot of violence; there's just a lot of things that you could pick up in the air. We didn't particularly see it all at this time, except the fear. The violence came later. At this point, it was mostly a lot of clerical work. They just typed up what they were charging us with and we were allowed to make a phone call, and naturally, we called our parents. We were told that we would have to go to central booking and then go see a judge.

From this time on it was really scary, because when they moved us from the precinct holding cell, we couldn't get to court until the next day, so they took us downstairs where they have individual cells. And when we got down there, it was a gray dungeon with bars. And they had a lot of people locked up down there. I forget how big it was; maybe twenty, thirty cells. Me and my friends were separated for the first time, and it stopped really being a joke. The cells were about five by eight feet. They stank. There was a wooden slat for a bed; there was a little porcelain toilet that was dirty connected to a sink in the rear. If you wanted water, they had this little plumbing thing where you flushed the toilet and you could get drinking water if you pushed the same button. I didn't use the toilet or drink any water the whole night.

I was just plain scared. The cell was cold. Graffiti everywhere. And before they put us in the cell, they took our shoestrings, our belts, our jackets. No pillow, no room service, no attention, no nothing. And all you hear all night is them bringing other guys in there and other guys making a lot of noise, and some guys talking through the bars to their friends on the outside. And one of the things that I just vividly remember was the keys. Every time the cop that was assigned down there brought somebody in, every time he walked, his keys would shake. I couldn't sleep anyway because I was so scared. I didn't know what was going on, what the procedure was. The cops were bored, because obviously they go through this day in and day out.

So I just sat in the cell and tried to figure out what was going to happen to me. I was finally going to jail—all these years of trying, I guess, and I finally succeeded, but on a bullshit charge. So this went on all night and I never did sleep. They got us up in the morning, and the only thing we had to eat or drink was a cup of coffee. And the cops kept complaining because they had to spend their money to go out and buy us some coffee. Detention in the precinct just doesn't come with any amenities. You know, you don't get anything. A lot of people were asking questions and the cop was just saying, "Shut the fuck up, man. I don't know—tell it to the judge. You'll see a lawyer—I don't know, I don't know, I don't know." So it was very isolated from that point on.

In the morning when they came to pick us up to go to court, we had to line up outside of our cells, and as they called off our names they handcuffed us to this long chain. And there were seven or eight guys per chain on both sides of the cells downstairs, so there were about fifteen, sixteen people going down to court. After they handcuffed us to the chain, they chained the two chains together and marched us outside to a paddy wagon. They locked us in there and then they drove us down to the Tombs. They made a stop at a couple of other local precincts to fill up the van, because there was a lot of guys going to court that morning. And you see guys from all over town who were getting busted for the third and fourth time who were just used to the routine. You know, it was sort of like a dead man's land. You're young and you're getting busted for the first time, where these guys are used to this routine. The van had no windows or anything and it's cold in the van, too; there's no heat, there's no light.

So we get down to the Tombs. We back in and we file out; we're still chained and handcuffed to each other. They walk us up a couple of flights of stairs and we go into a part that's called central booking. In every borough that I've ever been in, central booking is one of the dirtiest—I don't know, it's very destitute—I mean, it's just like a dirty atmosphere. The walls are dirty, there's a lot of graffiti, a lot of piss and urine. You smell that in everything. By this time, you're sort of getting used to the impersonal treatment. The people that you're dealing with are treating you just like a number or a face in the crowd. They see this every day. All you are is just a different face, same routine. They fill out some more paper and you're being handed over like a piece of property. The guy that brings you down has to get this piece of paper signed that he delivered you, and then they have to sign off that they received you. And you go upstairs and get your picture and fingerprints taken, and then they stick you in another holding cell somewhere. This cell is a little bit bigger than the holding cells in the precincts. There are maybe fifty, sixty, seventy guys in there. There are about three or four benches and one toilet; it's just this little porcelain thing you sit on, and it's supposed to be white, but it never is with so much dirt and grime on it.

The smell in those things is overwhelming; some of those guys have been there for a long time. Some of the guys don't take showers; when they were on the street they smelled like pigs. And there are always people coming in and coming out—these joints are never empty. And then there are bums and guys that are coming in just to get out of the street. They sleep there and they don't bathe. They don't clean and their smell just stays there; there's no air conditioning in there. So you're in there with all these nasty smells and all these different guys coming in, and you're starting to get the idea about the type of place you're in.

At this point, you've been searched and all your weapons are taken from you, but if you have any money or anything else, that's still in your pocket. And while you're in central booking, anybody that wants to play tough guy or what have you can. If you can't handle yourself, you're liable to get hurt and stuck up right there. I mean, not with a weapon, just

brute strength, intimidation. You have to wait in central booking until your fingerprints come back through the computer,
because some guys have a habit of getting arrested under
aliases and some guys have records and some guys don't.
What the courts want to know is if you have a previous
record, if there are any warrants out for you, and if you have
a prior criminal history. So until this information comes
back you have to sit right there in central booking and sometimes people sit there for days. I think that was my biggest
fear at that point: I would have to sit in here and watch these
guys come and go—that they would forget I was here and
I wouldn't get to see a judge.

I had called my mother, and she was waiting for me in
court, because they had given her a date and a time and a
court location where I would be. So I just wanted to hurry
up and get up there and see my mother; just see somebody
human and see some sunlight. After my prints finally did
come back, it took a couple of hours. Then they took us
upstairs to another location, which is like a holding cell—
actually it's a group of holding cells—on the floor that the
particular court is on. At this stage this is your first court
appearance, because you're going to get arraigned on the
charges against you. So you're in different holding cells. And
again, these little holding cells are like the big one that was
downstairs, because guys are constantly coming in and going
out. There's still a little bit of intimidation going on there,
but mainly it's a lot of rap and conversations, speculation
on what's going to happen when everyone gets their turn to
see the judge. And you hear a lot of stories and advice based
on what you tell these guys you were arrested for. The guys
that have been there before will usually tell you that you're
going to go home, or tell your legal aid this, and this is what'll
happen, and I know the judge; you know, you hear a lot of
stories.

It's at this point before you go see the judge that you'll
see a legal aid. Your name will be called and the guards will
take you out and you go to a little penned-in area where you
speak to a legal aid, who will usually tell you what's going
on. The legal aid asked me what happened and I explained
the situation. And he said that maybe he'll be able to talk

to the judge and get it knocked down to loitering or some other bullshit charge and maybe he'll just get me to walk. I had been arrested for attempted robbery and illegal entry. That was what I was being charged with at this time. I told him exactly what happened, and he's the one that told me that the cops write up more than they could substantiate because it looks better. And when you get to court, they'll usually plea bargain it down, because they don't want to take the time to go back and forth to court. And the case that I had was a meatball case, and he could probably get rid of this right away. Then he asked me if there's anybody I knew in the courtroom in case the judge wanted to get nasty and set some bail. So I told him my mother was there. He said it wasn't likely that they would set bail, and if they did want me to reappear in court they would probably release me on my own recognizance.

According to the legal aid, the police dealt with so many felonies and other violent criminal offenses that after I told him what happened he said, "I don't even know why they arrested you. It's a waste of time." I explained to him that we were just drinking wine and got curious; and when the fire engines pulled out, we just walked in and looked around. And we didn't have a record prior to that—this was my first arrest. The legal aid told me essentially what was going to happen: the DA was going to rant and rave but don't worry about it. They sent me back to the pen and I waited another couple of hours, and they finally called my case. The DA went through his spiel, my lawyer went through his, and the judge made his decision: I was acquitted and I walked out.

After two days in jail, I was glad to see my mom and to see some sunshine and daylight, because being locked up in all of these pens, you don't see any sunshine.

I'VE BEEN ARRESTED A TOTAL of maybe twenty to twenty-five times. All the times that I spent in jail were because I couldn't get bailed out or it was suggested that I not get bailed out at the time, because it would be a waste of money since at my court appearance I would be cut loose anyway. In addition to the Manhattan County Jail, I've been in the Brooklyn House of Detention. I've been in Bronx County Jail, which is the Bronx House of Detention for Men, Queens County Jail, Albany County Jail, Dutchess County Jail, Orange County Jail, and Rikers Island.

County jails are always set up the same way. You're locked in twenty-two, twenty-three hours out of the day. There aren't very many programs in the county jails because the population is always changing: you have different guys coming in and out. They're either getting bailed out or they're going to court and getting cut loose, or what have you. So there's not really much to do in county jail, except sit there and do your time or worry about how much time you're going to get in an upstate prison.

Except for Rikers Island, most county jails are small. They have little segments or little quarters—they call them blocks—where you go. They have some rough type of classification according to whatever you got arrested for. They try to separate criminals by their charge, but they don't succeed very well; and a lot of times you'll get kids locked in with adults because of lack of space or what have you. You go into what you call isolation for the first couple of days in the county jail while they go over the paper work; they want to make sure you're not suicidal or there are no more charges pending, or nobody else is coming to pick you up from another county, state or whatever. After you get through this, then they assign you to a cell block where you will remain until they dispose of your case.

ONE TIME BACK IN 1971, when I was twenty-four, I had gotten busted for grand larceny—I stole a camera. I had gone to court and I had been arraigned and I had the case taken care of at the arraignment. And it took me a day and a half to get to arraignment—you know, my prints had to come back from central booking. So I copped a plea to petit larceny and walked out of court. But still being an active dope fiend, I went to 166th Street on Teller Avenue in the Bronx. When I got busted they took the camera and everything, and they kept it the day I left jail. I didn't have any more money. I ran into this guy around the block on Teller Avenue and I told him I had just come out of jail. At this time, I was out of jail about a half an hour. He had a couple of dollars and he bought dope for me and him.

115

So we decided to go to this abandoned building on Teller Avenue. We get upstairs and we have only one set of works, so he got high first. We were in an empty apartment and we had put a couch and a stick up against the front door. Just as I was starting to inject the drugs and get high, there's all this banging and noise at the front door. I'm trying to figure out what's going on. They eventually kicked the door in and moved the couch. It was the TPF, the Tactical Police Force. They had followed us upstairs and came in to arrest us for using drugs and for possession of works. I tried to plead with them that I wasn't out forty-five minutes—I just came out of jail! But to no avail. These were highly spirited narcotics officers of the Tactical Police Force. And they were looking to make arrests and it didn't matter. Fortunately, I was able to get the case dismissed and beat the rap.

WHEN I GOT BUSTED FOR ROBBERY in 1981, which led to my only state prison time, I spent over a year in the New York City jail system before I was transferred to the upstate joints. This is how the bust happened. I had gone to stick up two numbers bankers in Riverdale. And it was really not necessary because my mother had just passed away six months before, and I was doing all right. I was playing in a Latin band and working as a counselor for ex-offenders. I was separated from my wife, and I had a four-room apartment with a separate room for my daughter, Kimberly. I had my drums, a good stereo system and a lot of material stuff. I had a couple of Gs in the bank, but for some reason I had just developed this lousy attitude. Things just didn't have the same meaning to me anymore. And I was drug-free at the time. I really didn't need the money, but I had started associating with some guys that were still into street life. And one of them had told me about this guy I used to work for, Manny, a numbers controller, but that Manny had stopped doing numbers and some other Spanish guy had taken over; and how he's got big money and he's not connected with anybody, and how they were thinking about sticking him up.

So I let the thought run through my mind for a couple of weeks. I don't know, one day I just got up and decided that I was going to do it. I drove up to Riverdale, I parked the car, I knocked on the door this time, and I didn't use a mask or anything. When the first guy opened the door—I never knew who he was, it never came to trial—I shoved a gun in his face, pushed him back and closed the door. I said, "Man, take me upstairs where the money is." We walked up the stairs and there's a lot of rooms in this big house; it was similar to the one where I had stuck up the other numbers bankers the last time. There was an accounting room, adding machines, money, everything. I went through the same thing: I tied them up and opened the safe. They had the money counted and packed in the safe in like eight bundles, so I took that. There was also a couple of bundles on the table, five Gs, and some money spread out. I estimated there was about $88,000, and I stuffed it in a little school bag I had and I left.

But what happened was—again, it's a white neighborhood—some lady from across the street had seen me when I walked into the neighborhood, and thought that I came into the neighborhood to burglarize. I found out this later through my lawyer. So she decided to call the police to say there's a black prowler in the neighborhood. She didn't know or have any idea of what I came here for or what I was going to do. I mean, I purposely walked up to where I was going. I stuck them up, and I was walking my way out of the neighborhood after throwing the gun down the sewer. And that's when the cops came down on me.

The cop car screeched up in front of me, they jumped out and had their guns out: "Freeze!" So I looked and I started to run, but then I hesitated, and by that time some of the other squad cars had pulled up. They took my bag, handcuffed me, and put me in the back of the car. They didn't take me to the precinct right away. Somehow or other, they had gotten the information of what house I came out of and they went back into the house. So I'm sitting in the squad car and I'm thinking, "Goddamn! Now they're going to have me for kidnapping, robbery, and all this other shit." The cops come back out and they're talking among themselves and I'm still sitting in the car. They have the bag of money in the front. So about an hour later I'm taken to the precinct. None of them are talking to me and I'm trying to find out what I'm charged with. So I'm talking and someone told me to shut up. We get inside and I overhear two Hispanic cops laughing and talking: "Yeah, this crazy fucker went and stuck up _____." I forgot the guy's name. "Well, this is where we get our money from — can you imagine this guy, the heart of this guy to come in here and fuck with our money?" They're saying this right in front of me in Spanish not knowing that I'm Cuban and I speak Spanish.

Now I'm starting to wonder what the hell is going on, because they're not charging me or writing out any arrest report. Finally, about three hours later, one of the other cops comes in and takes me out of the holding tank; he takes me into the room, sits me down, puts a paper in front of me and says, "Sign it!"

I say, "I ain't signing shit."

He says, "Look, let me explain something to you; you're getting a break right now. We could be getting you for kidnapping, armed robbery."

I say, "Man, I didn't have any weapon."

He says, "Fuck that, we could still get you for armed robbery." And he lays out a bunch of other charges. And he says, "I don't know whether you know it or not, but the people that you ran into have influence and they decided not to press charges. But because it was reported and recorded we're going to have to charge you with something. So this is the deal. Shut the fuck up, sign this paper, and face a burglary charge."

So I looked at him and I thought about it for a little bit and I hemmed and hawed, and we bullshitted for a little while. And finally, I saw that it would be to my advantage if I did just what he said. The money was never reported. So that $88,000 just went right out the window. I ended up being indicted for burglary in the third degree. I copped out to attempted burglary in the second degree and was sentenced to one to three years.

I don't know for sure but I'd say the guys I robbed must have been police-protected numbers bankers. From dealing with the system, and from knowing how certain things go down, nine times out of ten what you're charged with when you get arrested is not what you get indicted for. The court or your lawyer will break it down. But the more good felony arrests a patrolman or a detective has, the better his chance of promotion. This should have been a damn good bust for the police. There's no way in the world that when a cop makes an arrest he isn't going to charge you with the most serious felony offenses. To bust me for what I got arrested for, and for me to cop out to what I copped out to, I mean, somebody had to say something to somebody. There's no way, I mean, with the amount of police activity that was involved and the reports and everything else. I don't know what happened to the $88,000. I'd say the police probably split it up. I haven't got it, property hasn't got it, and it's not on any sheet that the money was confiscated.

When I went to court the first time for arraignment, they hit me with $35,000 bail, which I thought was ridiculous. I couldn't get out, so there was no sense in even dealing with that. I stayed in the Bronx County Jail going back and forth to court for about four months. And while I was in Bronx County—I was up on the seventh floor—I was up there with some guys that got busted on a couple of homicides and they had decided that they were going to break out. They didn't want to stay in Bronx County Jail.

So one day we had recreation, and when you have rec they lock out everybody on the tier. We get an hour's recreation out of our cells. They have a gym and a music room there, but you have your choice for that hour of rec. At this one point, all seven guys were locked out, and there are only two guards on that particular tier. So some guy snatched a guard, beat him up pretty bad, threw him in a cell and took his uniform and keys. But looking back, it wasn't really very well planned, because they only had one set of keys and that was to that first door into the cell block. There's still another door.

I was planning on getting out with them. I didn't know how much time I was facing; I wanted to get out too. But when they found out that all they had was one set of keys, they had to wait for another guard to come around. And the plan at that point was to snatch that guard and take his keys. But what happened was that when another guard did come around he knocked on the door and the inmate that had taken the guard's clothes opened the peep hole in the door to see who it was, and he was going to open the door and let the guard in. But the CO (correctional officer) saw that the person in uniform was not the CO in charge of the block and put out the alarm. About fifteen minutes later, a riot squad came in there and they started kicking ass. I mean, they were beating everybody in there—and there were only seven of us out. Everybody got beat up, even those inmates who weren't attempting to escape. They were just swinging sticks and kicking ass. I didn't get seriously hurt, but two of the other inmates did. They sent them to Bellevue Hospital. Eventually, they separated everybody that was on that particular cell block. They sent me and another guy to Rikers Island. They sent some guys to Brooklyn House of Detention and some other guys to Queens.

By this time I had gotten used to going to court, which was a hassle because you'd have to get up at 5:30 in the morning and you'd go downstairs to these big holding cells that they had, and they would get everybody all over the county jail. Bronx County Jail is big: about eight hundred to twelve hundred inmates are in there. And on an average day over half of them are going to court. The big problem is the paperwork. You're there until about 9:00, 10:00 in the morning until transportation arrives. And as they call your name, they handcuff you, put you on a little chain line again, and take you downstairs to the buses, the paddy wagons. By the time you get to court, it's about 11:00, 11:30; you've got to check in the court. And it's miserable, man, because there's nothing but a lot of bodies. Buses are coming in from every institution around the city, because guys would get busted in one borough, they'll house them in another borough, and some guys have gotten rearrested; so they all have to come to this borough for a court case, and all you're doing is seeing a bunch of guys all over again.

You have to wait until the guy comes downstairs, calls your name, and takes you still handcuffed upstairs to another holding pen on the floor that your court is on. People who have to go to court who are free on bail or their own recognizance are on the other side. If you have to go to court and you're detained, there's another doorway that you go through, and there are always guards around. So for weeks and months guys are being shuffled back and forth like cattle, just herded here and herded there. And anytime you're in some place where there's a space, you're handcuffed and chained to the next guy.

WHEN I GOT TRANSFERRED from Bronx County after the escape attempt, they sent me to Rikers Island, so I was going back and forth to court from there. Rikers Island is a city prison that's on an island. It's got around 12,000 or 13,000 inmates. Because of the overcrowded conditions, the first night I spent in Rikers Island was in a dormitory, which I hated. I was really scared in that dormitory since there are no bars separating guys, and what goes on inside of a prison that size is like the same shit that goes on in the streets. You've got your bullies, you've got your cliques, you've got your gangs. And it's a big wide open space, so you can't hide. You're not always there to be able to watch over what little property that you have. And if somebody or a gang decided that they want to take what you got, there isn't much you can do about it.

The part of the jail that I went to was an old brick building. It was called the House of Detention for Men. And if you've ever seen any of those old James Cagney movies, that's just what Rikers Island looks like. Each block has two sides, the A side and the B side. And basically, what it is are cinder blocks with cells on the inside. And in each block, there are 619 cells, and there are four COs guarding these guys. There's a bathroom area with eight urinals and eight toilets, again with no tops on them. And there are eight shower spigots in the back. There are no partitions. You may be taking a shit, and they can check you out. You take a shower, it's the same thing. So I stayed in Rikers Island for about nine months, because I was going back and forth to fight my case.

I was living in B block. And at this time, Rikers Island was like being in New York City. I mean, there were drugs— heroin, cocaine—and we made wine, so getting high was not difficult to do. And it was easy to smuggle drugs inside Rikers Island, man, there should have been a law against it! There was this one young white guy, David, who was from Long Island. He had been busted for drugs, and he was waiting to go to trial. And David's old lady—his wife—used to smuggle heroin into Rikers Island to him. But David was okay—I guess about as friendly as you can get in a prison setting. He didn't do favors for everybody, but he turned on a few people. There was one black guy that he used to turn on all the time. He was a strong black guy and he kept the other guys off of David, because David was white and he was weak. But because he was supplying this other guy with heroin from time to time, David got protection. And every once in a while, as heroin users are prone to do, you'll turn other people on if you've got enough. You know, heroin makes you friendly; heroin makes you do anything. So he wasn't really a bad guy, and it wasn't that he didn't want to turn on everybody, because he was the kind of guy that would have. But you have to understand, he's in jail now, and he just didn't have enough dope to turn on 366 different guys. So he picked and chose who he turned on, which was fine—it was his drugs.

But one day, this guy named Bruno was down from the maximum-security joint in Dannemora on a review of his sentence. He had gotten forty years to life on a manslaughter conviction, and he was down in Rikers Island on appeal. But Bruno had a nasty attitude. He was black, but not too many people liked him. Nobody really liked him. Bruno was like one of these rock solid guys; he used to work out all the time, and he used that size to intimidate people. He just had a fucked-up attitude. He thought he was a bad ass, the toughest guy in the institution. So one day Bruno went to David and told him that he was going to start taking over David's heroin. He told David to tell his old lady to bring in some dope for him, and how much. And David told him he couldn't do that. The only reason Bruno didn't kick David's ass then was because there was a lot of guys around. So Bruno bided his time.

By this time, I had been sentenced and I was just waiting to go back upstate to start doing my time. One day I was in court and when I came back, I found out that they had thrown Bruno off the third floor tier. Because Bruno went down to David and, oh man, he blackened his eyes, broke a couple of bones, since David refused to bring the dope in for him. And like two minutes later, TK—the guy who used to lock in next to me—got together with five or six other guys that David used to share drugs with; and they dragged Bruno out of his cell, took him upstairs to the closed-off third floor tier, broke his leg, and threw him off the tier. His back was broken. The last I heard he was paralyzed. But he learned, and nobody was sorry, not even the guards. Nobody got arrested for that, nobody got charged. He slipped. He slipped and fell.

AT FIRST THEY OFFERED ME a cop-out: seven and half to fifteen years. I told them to kiss my ass. So they sent me back and gave me another court date. I waited another month and went back to court. And my lawyer and the DA would wheel and deal, and it came down to five to ten. Well, the five to ten was an illegal sentence and we had to go back and fight with that because this was my first time; and when you get sentenced the first time it's always in triples: one to three, three to nine, six to eighteen, seven to twenty-one. It's a technicality, but sometimes you get caught up in it. So I had to go back to court to not accept the illegal sentence. Then they came down and offered me four to twelve, then three to nine. So I just hung on and waited it out. I didn't have anything to lose.

I played until I got offered one to three, and they were very adamant about that; either take the one to three or take it to trial. I was tempted to take it to trial because of the particular circumstances associated with my arrest, but my lawyer was telling me there's no way that I could prove that the police were in collusion with the bankers in the illegal numbers and that if I did take it to trial, I would lose. So I played the waiting game, but my lawyer said that I should take the one to three that they were going to give me. I got a great deal of help from the lawyer that was assigned to represent me. I could have gotten more time; he could have just done like a lot of other legal aids and said, "We'll cop out to this—it's better" and this and that; and me not knowing any better, I would have done it. My lawyer fought for me. So when he told me that this one to three was the bottom line, I took it.

From Rikers Island they sent me to Sing Sing; from Sing Sing to Downstate; from Downstate to Clinton; from Clinton to Attica; from Attica back down to Clinton, and then to a minimum-security prison. All together, I served about three years and some change in custody before I was paroled.

8

CHAPTER

BEHIND PRISON WALLS

THE DAY I COPPED OUT IN COURT I belonged to the state. I was supposed to go to the Downstate Correctional Facility for classification, but because of overcrowding they sent me first to Sing Sing, the Ossining Correctional Facility. From the time you leave the city institution when you get on the bus, you're handcuffed and in leg irons and shackles. You can't move. The thought that stayed on my mind was, what would happen if we crossed the bridge and the bus fell into the water? We would drown. The guards aren't going to come back and unloosen all the shackles. The first thing I remember approaching Sing Sing was the thirty-foot high concrete walls and gun towers—guns everywhere—and I was scared. I was really scared. All the stories start going through my head, and all the guys in the bus going up there with you are telling you stories; you don't know what to believe. So we passed through the first gate. And I kind of knew it was final; there was no getting out of here, because the gates are huge. It was like going into a dark tunnel, like a theater for the forgotten, because you're entering a world of hopelessness and uselessness.

And everybody handled you as if you were a thing. You're not treated like a person anymore. From the time that you've been convicted and sentenced to your state time, your name is no longer yours—it's replaced by a number. Mine was 82A0932, and even the time I was out on parole, that's what I was known by. From that time on, you no longer have a name. Your number is your name, and you'd better remember it; because even when they call you for visits, or over the loud speakers, or anything, they call those numbers; they don't call names.

The first thing they do is give you a haircut. You're not in the barber chair for two or three minutes; they just cut off all of your hair. Then you go to an area where you're strip-searched. You take off all your clothes. And there are about eight, nine, ten of us in a row; and for each guy there's a guard standing right in front of you. They look through your hair, they look through your nose, they open your mouth, they make you bend over, they look in your ass. They even have rubber gloves now; they stick their fingers in your ass; they probe. From there you take a shower, what can be called a shower. The first thing you realize is that millions of people have gone this way before you, and millions of people are going to come this way after you. You know, nothing is yours, nothing is personal. At this point you're naked—not just without clothes but I mean without anything or anybody.

Nothing is private. The shower room is a big open space with spigots and there's no room for modesty or anything else. And at the same time you have other inmates that have already been there looking at you, glaring at you, making comments: "Punk, you gonna be mine, you gonna be my wife" and I'm going to take this, I'm going to take that. So you come out of the shower. It's hard to feel clean in a situation like that, but you get used to it because nobody wants to hear your complaints anyway, and nobody's going to do anything about it. So along with everything else there's the feeling of helplessness.

They give you a towel and you see a doctor. The doctor is another letdown and a disappointment, because you don't get a real physical. You get the idea that he's going to see a million guys today and there's no personal treatment. By this time, you're sort of longing to be treated as a person, as an individual. But that's not happening; he just looks at you and asks if there's anything wrong. And he checks

through whatever medical records you have to that point and
he asks you if you want to see a doctor or if you think you
have problems; if not—next. They issue you clothes and
again, there are no particulars. The guys look at you and they
throw clothes at you: two sets of green pants, two green
shirts, a pair of prison shoes and a bag. And you go sit in
another area. And when they have enough guys, they take
you inside the prison proper.

New guys coming in—fish or whatever you want to call
them—are always taken to either A block or B block in Sing
Sing. Each block has six tiers or six floors of cells. And there
are forty-one cells on each side of each floor. There is one
gigantic cell block internally divided into sections or cells.
And surrounding the cells are wire mesh fence and high concrete walls. It's like bird cages. There are only three colors
in there: blood red, gray and green, and they're very dull and
very drab colors. The windows are maybe twenty yards away
from the cells. We don't have control over them; the guards
open them and close them as they see fit. There's not very
much sunlight coming in; the windows are dirty and grimy
and the whole place is just painted desolate.

WHEN I WAS IN PRISON at this time, I didn't use drugs because
nothing is free in prison—you pay for everything. And I had
gotten hip real, real quick. I didn't want to be in anybody's
debt, because one of my fears was that I would eventually
have to pay off in sex, and I didn't want to get involved in
that at all. And I had seen what had happened to a lot of guys
who couldn't pay their debts. I didn't have a dime. And I had
already come to understand that my dope habit would have
gotten me in a lot of trouble. Dope was expensive on the
street; it was twice as expensive in prison.

The first two or three days after I was arrested and put
in county jail, I went through withdrawal. After that, I had
residual side effects for the first couple of weeks. But by the
time I had gotten to prison, I had been in police custody for
over a year, so whatever the physical effects of my dope habit,
my body had already adjusted. Yet I was always shooting
dope in my head. Every day I got high mentally. Every day.
That's all I wanted to do; I just wanted to get high. And of

course, there was no adequate drug counseling when I came through the system in 1981, 1982. They didn't think drugs were really a problem. Not that they really cared. Some guys were sentenced to programs; you know, they had to go to AA or NA or go to some type of therapy for the drugs or alcohol, but it's really bullshit. I had found out what was going on in the system. The people that were working in there really didn't give a shit about more than just coming in and picking up their paycheck. The more work they had to do, the more pissed off they got. So if you just came in and didn't give them any problems, they were more than glad to sign whatever piece of paper it was that you had gone through some treatment program.

Downstate Prison is where inmates are first sent for classification; and when you get sent there you see a counselor. They classify you according to your crime and how much time you got. And this classification sticks with you throughout your time in prison. Not that it really means anything, because you go where they have the space for you. So when I left Downstate, I was sent to a maximum-security institution. They recommended that I have an academic program or that I learn a vocational trade. And they suggested I continue my education. See, they didn't know that I was kicking a dope habit because I had gotten busted for attempted burglary. Even though I had a drug sheet, this particular charge did not have any narcotics connected with it. And I didn't tell my counselor anything, because I knew that they would get me caught up in going through these goddamn programs and all this other stuff, and I didn't want to hear about it. And I didn't want to have to become restricted. A lot of guys that are strung out go into prison, and they don't want to hear about rehab. They don't want to hear about recovery, about AA and NA. They're not ready to kick.

And I didn't want to have my parole or my release tied up to me going to some damn program. I didn't want to go through these programs and hear some counselor talking to me about drugs and about things being good on the outside, when I really didn't have a home to go back to. My mother had died, I didn't have any clothes, I didn't have anything. I just wasn't in the mood for that. I was more concerned with getting hard and surviving this prison thing. And I didn't feel that all this drug therapy crap was going to do it for me, so I didn't want to get caught up in that.

IN THE BEGINNING, probably my biggest problem of adjustment was dealing with the intermittent violence and not really knowing other inmates. I remember I was going to lunch one day in Sing Sing, and this guy was walking in front of me. I didn't pay too much attention to him. We had locked out on my tier, and we were going down to chow hall. When we got to the stairs, this one guy shoved his way in front of me. I was getting ready to say something to him — actually, I was going to hit him — but something told me not to. I hesitated, which is bad because in prison that might be all the advantage somebody else needs to harm you. But I was glad I hesitated this time, because he stabbed a guy that was in front of me. And he kept walking, the stabbed guy fell down the stairs, and I kept walking. It wasn't any of my business. I went on to chow. I ate my food and that was it.

Another time, I was taking a shower, and this big black bruisy dude comes to the front of the shower stall. The showers in Sing Sing are like cells. It's the same size as the cell, but instead of having a bed and a toilet in there, it has a spigot for a shower. And your cell is like your home. Anybody that comes to your cell has to stay outside and wait for your permission before he can enter. Anybody that goes in your cell without your permission is in automatic violation: you know, he's robbing you. That's grounds for kicking his ass. So when I was taking a shower and this big bruisy guy came to the shower stall — him and a friend — once he crossed the line to step into the shower, I knew what was happening. He thought I was soft and he was going to come in there and take my ass. And I had already figured this out, so I had dropped the state soap that I was washing with, and I looked at him, and he kept advancing inside the shower. State soap is as hard as concrete brick. It chafes your skin and everything else, but it's the only thing you have to wash with.

So I bent over to pick up the soap and I had my wash-cloth in my hand; and I wrapped the washcloth around the soap so I could get a better grip on it. When I came up off the ground, I busted him right in his jaw. I hit him five or six times. I couldn't knock him out because he was too big, but I hurt him enough to knock him flat on his ass. "Every time you think about fucking with me, man, this is what you're going to have to think about." And I stepped outside the shower and I smacked the shit out of the dude that was with him. And then I walked back to my cell. But essentially what I told him was that I might not be as big as you are, but I'm a little crazy, and if you think you can just take me or my body because you want sex or whatever, that's bullshit. And I told his friend that he was a punk and a sissy, because I smacked him, I didn't hit him. You punch a man, you smack a woman. So they got my message.

In prison I developed a reputation of being a bit crazy. I had to, because like they say out in the street, God protects crazy people and babies. In prison he does the same thing. And if people can't predict what you'll do or say at any given moment, they think about that. The stronger guys don't have too many problems because their size intimidates a lot of people. But I learned about big guys, too. They're not as flexible. They might be strong, which means you just don't get too close, or you don't get caught. Or you hit him hard, quick, first. But a crazy guy, you never know when he'll go off, or what he'll do to you, or when he'll do it. Eventually, I got big. I blew up to 209 pounds lifting weights and eating plenty of starches—and I wasn't fat. Before that happened, though, I played the crazy role, which wasn't really too hard in prison.

Once in Downstate while I was waiting for classification, I had gotten a job as a porter mopping the tiers in the cell block. And I used to bring toilet paper and other articles to the different guys because they were locked in. So one guy would want me to bring a magazine to his buddy on another tier, and I'd bring it over there. One night, I guess he had gotten used to me being his personal maid and he wanted me to do something. And it was the way he asked me. I told him he'd have to wait. So he goes off: "Fuck you, man, what you mean I got to wait? I'll kick your ass." Since he was locked behind the cell, I just walked up to his cell and said, "Listen, man, there's no sense in me and you arguing right now because you can't get out and I can't get in. But when we lock out for breakfast in the morning, we'll take care of all this bullshit. In the meantime, don't ask me for shit, because you ain't getting nothing tonight, and if you don't have any toilet paper, you're going to have to wipe your ass with that magazine."

When we locked out in the morning, I'm standing there in line, and the guy that used to lock all my tiers—his name is Alex—was in the line next to me. So the other guy comes down off of his tier. He walks past me and he's staring at me—and I'm staring at him. Then he walks behind me and he stands there in the line. And he just keeps looking at me, you know, like he's supposed to intimidate me by looking at me. So I just turn around and looked at my buddy Alex and Alex looked at me, as if to say, "Go ahead and do what you got to do." So I said, "Fuck it." I turned around and said, "Man, you can look at me all you want, but you put your big stupid-ass hands on me, I'll knock you out." Oh, man! He starts jumping up and down and yelling and going back toward the day room, which is like a TV room; it's like our rec room. He's going through all of this acting and jumping up and down, and takes off his jacket. So while he's taking off his jacket—when he's got his jacket half off—I locked up his arms. And I turned around and punched him five or six times. I knocked him out. Knocked him right out. And he's laying there and the guards come over. And I was ready for them, too, because I didn't care.

So I was ready for the COs to come jumping all over me, and they didn't, which surprised me. A black CO named Brownie just walked over to me and told me to get back in line. And he said, "If you didn't kick his ass, I was going to write you up." I said, "All right, that's cool." But the white CO that was working there had reported it. So Brownie came back to me later on that night and explained to me what happened. Well, they took my job away, which pissed me off. I was the porter—a runner—and I got paid sixty cents a day. I used to clean and mop and sweep, which meant I could lock out of my cell. While everybody else is locked in, I'm running around, you know, which I liked to do. I didn't get any solitary time or anything for that fight, but they took my job.

In prison, you have to have eyes in the back of your head, in your feet. You've got to have eyes all around you. The one thing that I was fearful of is that you never know what another man is thinking of at any given point. Even your friends might be okay one day and fucked up the next day. You know, there's a lot of things you do and there's a lot of things you don't do in prison. I don't play with anybody with my hands; I don't go boxing around or hitting people. I don't walk into anybody's cell. And when I see people, and I sense that they're in a different frame of mind, I don't go near them, I don't talk to them.

When I got to Clinton Correctional Facility in Dannemora—a maximum-security joint—I was locking out for recreation one day. I was walking down the tier, and something just told me to turn around. It was just something that I felt, like a vibration. I turned around and here's this guy with a pipe and he's going to hit me on the head with it. So as he's bringing the pipe down, I blocked it and it tore open my arm. But I had gone through a little martial arts, and I caught his arm, hooked it, and locked it into my right forearm, and then I just pushed with my left arm and I broke his arm. By that time, I was beyond caring about other people. I just kept stomping on him and kept hitting him. You know, I just wanted to tear his body up.

Later somebody told me, very vaguely, something about his old lady. He thought that I was seeing his old lady in the outside world. And it turned out that he was just mistaken. I just looked like the guy seeing his wife. He was carrying around all this hatred for him. And since I was only in the prison about two weeks—and only in that cell block for about two days—I was fairly new; and this guy had already been in Clinton for like seven years. I got sixty days in the hole, which is solitary confinement. They throw you in a concrete environment; there's no clothes, no heat. They give you a bucket to shit and piss in and that's it, for sixty days. And they give you bread and water. They slip it through the opening; sometimes you might get a half-assed decent meal, sometimes you might not.

IN PRISON, THERE'S A LOT OF boredom, because all you have is time to think. Even when you go into the programs. When you come from classification, they give you a list of things they want you to do, how they want you to program, how they want you to spend your day. When you get to a regular state facility—maximum, medium, or minimum—they give you duty assignments according to your classification. If they want you to go to school, they try to set up a school program for you. If they want you to go to work, they try to set up that type of program. Most of the work is make-do work, kill-time work. I mean, it's not challenging, complicated, or anything else; it's just menial work to do while you're in there. Working in the metal shop or working on the machines. The machines do the work; there's nothing complicated. Or working in the laundry—all you do is wash clothes. Working in the kitchen—all you're doing is washing tables and dishes.

These jobs don't equip you to make a living when you get out. They don't equip you for anything. Even in some of the more technically advanced jobs, you're using old equipment, old systems, old ways of doing things. In the outside world, technology has advanced a hundred years by the time you get out. Most of the equipment that's inside these institutions had been donated by other industries and companies; and this is the stuff that they can't get rid of, so they give it to the penitentiary and they write it off as a tax write-off. So you're learning an antiquated skill; even at the time that you're learning it, it's already out of date.

ONE DAY I CAME HOME from one of the programs and I found some cigarettes on my bed. Everybody in prison has to have a little hustle. The guys that work in the kitchen steal food and sell it. The guys that work in the laundry steal sheets, and that kind of stuff. The guys that work on the pants, they do alterations, but you pay for that. Some guys have people outside that send them money for cigarettes, commissary, this and that. I didn't have any of that, and I like to smoke and I like to eat a lot of food, but I didn't have any money. But I learned quick; I don't ask anybody for anything in prison.

The cigarettes and cookies on the bed—the old inmates will do that. And you walk in your cell, and you see cigarettes and you light them up. But then somebody comes along and says, "Yo, man, you got to pay for them cigarettes." You say, "I found those cigarettes on my bed, they're mine." They say, "That's bullshit—I put them there, they're mine. You owe me." What are you going to do, call the police? Not in the penitentiary. One of their favorite ways of extracting payments is either forcing you to get the money or taking it out of your ass—homosexual sex. And they do that. I didn't really know the rules at the time, but I knew enough not to smoke or do anything with something that wasn't mine; so I left it there on the bed. Actually, I quit smoking for a while, because I couldn't afford to pay the price. I didn't have the money, and I wasn't giving up any ass.

Sex turns into almost a physical force when you get in prison. You become more or less preoccupied with it, just like you do with TV programs that you can no longer see, people that you can no longer be with, clothes that you can no longer wear. Sex becomes excessive to the point that you have to have it. You've got to have a sexual release. There's really no control on your sexual release when you're in prison. Most guys tend to deviate. You have a lot of booty bandits—guys that just want that sexual release; and the object of their release gets perverted. And they don't care who they stick what into. These guys become fully obsessed with this. And new guys that come, you know, they just look at them as females.

One young white kid came in—it was in Clinton—and he looked soft; he looked kind of feminine. He'd never had any kind of homosexual experience prior to coming to prison. I think he got busted for some reefer, a lot of reefer. He got a light sentence, like one to three. But when you go out of segregation, which is where they keep you in any state prison for about two weeks to get you adjusted to being in prison, you're in the regular prison population. And you're an open target for other guys that are already in there. You know, they've been there for a while and you're coming into their house. And they can smell fear. All the inmates can smell fear. They're like predators, they start quick.

Me and this guy and a bunch of other guys were walking on our tier to our cells, and I heard some other bigger guys, black guys, saying, "Listen, man, that kid is soft, he's gonna be my punk. He's gonna be my woman." And I heard it a couple of times and they were referring to this other white kid. About three days later, I was going back to my cell. And as I was walking up the stairs, I saw five guys surround the kid. He started crying, and he was pleading with them not to do anything, but they just took him and threw him in the cell. Put a blanket over the foot of the cell so the guards couldn't see it and they just started tearing his ass open. There wasn't anything he could do. Nothing. If the guards did hear his screaming, they didn't give any notice. Their attitude is: as long as they aren't trying to break out, and as long as the guards don't have any special arrangement with this particular individual, they don't give a fuck. We're considered animals, man; we'll kill ourselves anyway.

The kid could have requested protective custody, but he didn't. So they turned him out, turned him into a person to be used and abused for homosexual sex. He became public property. A dude would make the kid give up his ass for some other favors that he'd want from somebody else, and in return he'd lend them his "girlfriend." So it was really a hopeless situation. A kid like this isn't strong enough to be on his own. Sometimes a weak guy might align himself with some other powerful inmate—give up his ass to him—but at least he'd keep the rest of the predators off him. You have some queens in prison who don't have a man. You know, it's just like prostitutes out in the street. Some work for pimps, some work on their own. But those are the strong ones, the strong queens. Because there's always somebody trying to jump on them all the time. I've had some guys think about going after me, but I discouraged that shit right away. That's when I went into my crazy act. And I let it be known wherever I went that I don't play that shit. I'm not gay, and if you're thinking of taking my ass, here's something else for you to think about: I will take you out.

There are some inmates that I know personally who did revert to homosexual activity while they were in prison. But outside of prison—before and after—they revert back to heterosexual behavior. One guy tried to explain it to me: he said it's a sexual need that he has, and since he can't get it the regular way, he'll deal with the homosexuality just so he can get his sex thing off.

In prison, you have to be careful where you go, what you say, and who you talk to, because there's always a different connotation placed on it. I remember one night back in Sing Sing when I first got there. Since we were new, we had to eat separate from the prison population. And I was sitting down eating, and this faggot came up and sat down at my table and started talking to me. So I was being nice — I was talking to him — but after he left, a buddy of mine that was in the escape attempt at Bronx County ran up to me and he said, "Man, don't do that no more."

I said, "What you talking about, I'm just sitting here eating."

He said, "Don't do that. Do you see that other guy back there in the kitchen? He wants to kill you right now for talking to his bitch."

I said, "What you talking about, man?" What happened was, the gay guy saw me and wanted to rap to me, but the guy that he was seeing before was this big bruisy black dude, and he was heavy and big and ugly, and I didn't want any part of that. But they get possessive about the guys that play those games. They get possessive about their women. And I had walked into a situation not knowing, and I could have been killed.

You have a lot of guys in prison that need to be in control — to dominate weaker people — but they will also be that way outside of prison. They want to maintain that dominant position and this might be their personal way of affirming themselves and their masculinity. Also, with a lot of black inmates violating white inmates, they're telling off white society — they're fucking white society by screwing the soft little white boy. So they're taking out their frustrations on the white society on this one little white individual. In the prisons I've been in, probably near 85 or 90 percent of the inmates are black or Hispanic. And they take out some of their frustrations toward whites this way, because there's still an imbalance in prison, too. Even though the whites are the minority, the majority of them are still in the powerful positions. Like, they get all the luxuries. They get TVs, they get the good jobs. So it's the same unequal society inside prison as it is outside.

INMATES HATE GUARDS—we call them bulls, hacks, COs, shit-heads, police—because the guards don't show compassion; they don't show anything else. In my experience, most guards are sadistic individuals. If they don't have a hate for inmates, especially black or Hispanic or poor inmates, when they start the job, they develop one. A lot of guards don't even want to touch inmates. They talk at them, not to them. They present that superiority gap: I'm better than you, I'm watching you. I am God as far as you're concerned, because I have the key to your cell. You jump when I say jump.

Some of these guards are just as rotten as we are, and the only difference between them and us is the color of our uniforms. We wear green, they wear blue. They go home at the end of an eight hour shift, we have to live there. The color difference in uniforms means they can always say, "I'm not like that. I don't wear a green uniform. I'm not in jail. I don't do the kind of shit that they do." But yet, if they were to go home and examine their own lifestyles—or their own lives—the similarities would knock their socks off.

Some of the guards are stealing all the time. They bring stuff home—clothes, supplies, equipment. In Sing Sing, guards are stealing jewelry. Sometimes prisoners are lucky enough to slip through with some jewelry on, a chain, a ring, or whatever. By the time you get into the state system—to Sing Sing or Downstate—you should have been stripped and all your personal items taken. Certain inmates are allowed to wear certain things. And after you're in the system for a while, you're allowed to get certain things delivered to you. Guards take things out of the package room all the time. People send up clothes, leather coats, especially the guys from New York City. After you've been in the system for a while, the only thing green that you have to wear is your pants. You can wear shirts, shoes, sneakers, you know, civilian stuff. But you have to wear green pants. Sometimes you can get sweaters and jackets. You never know when it's coming in. And the record keeping is so sloppy, it's easy for anything to get lost. Guards take money. They take jewelry. They take clothes. They take stuff from inside the prison—paper, typewriters.

Most guards have to become dehumanized to a point,

because in order to get their job, they're told that all they are is a watcher or a keeper. And it's kind of hard to relate to somebody in a nonhuman way. You're in a very vulnerable situation; and any contact of a positive nature—anything, man—is something that's needed. But you learn early that the COs do not give this up. You know, they're like machines. And all they do is tell you what to do, push you here and make you do that, and that's it. And they laugh at you. They try to make your stay as miserable as possible. They take their own frustrations out on you.

When I got to a minimum-security prison, there were some decent guards. I guess because the pressure wasn't really that much there, and most of the COs were local guys. They got to respect me and we developed a respectable relationship. A minimum-security prison is a little looser, as opposed to a maximum joint. So they got to know different sides of you. I wasn't a hardass like a lot of other New York inmates, you know, "fuck them and fuck the guards," and this and that. I mean, I had that in the back of my head, but I'll treat a man like he treats me. Not that I was kissing their ass or doing any of that, because I wasn't. But I had to live there. At the minimum joint there are no bars or anything there. So I guess the control dynamics were a little different. The COs at that point are more or less like counselors, really. Not one-on-one counselors, but like camp counselors trying to keep the group together. And the COs who are running the blocks have to keep the peace there. Because if they couldn't keep peace in their blocks they also got transferred. Being in the minimum joint, and having it like that, is a sweet job for a guard, because they don't do anything. All they have to do is tell us to clean up and do this and do that, and they can chill out.

Plus, being the editor of the newspaper, I got to talk to a lot of guards. A lot of them I still hated. A lot of them belong in the maximum joints, because they have a maximum-joint attitude. As editor of the prison newspaper they saw me not as this dumb nigger from New York, but as a black man who's intelligent, who's made a mistake, and who's paid his dues. And a lot of them related to that.

THE MOST POWERFUL LEADERS in any institution are the long-term guys or the lifers. When you get to the max joints, you get guys that are doing life. They are a strong clique. But the leadership is really fragmented, because prison life is broken down first of all along racial lines. And within those racial lines you have further divisions. You have the con bosses of each individual ethnic group. You have the black boss. You have the Italian boss. You have the Indian boss. And within those subgroups, you have things broken down further because you have different types of groups. In the black community, you have Muslims, you have guys from New York. It's even broken down to geographical areas: you have guys from New York City, you have guys from different cities in New York State, you have Jamaicans. And each one of these groups has a strong person—a leader—who you go to for things. First you go to the leader of your small group, and in turn, he goes to the leader of the broader group, and up the pyramid of influence and power. And then you have renegades. You know, guys of whatever color that are just bad.

In Attica and Clinton you have the mob forces. There were a couple of these organized crime Mafia guys in Attica and Clinton. And if they like you, it doesn't matter what color you are. The mob guys got treated real good. They had their own runners. They had cells that were more or less customized—carpets, color TV. And they run their own community just like they run gangs on the street. Everything from having somebody hit to distributing retribution to get something done. I had a guy that used to live in the next cell to mine. When I met Tommy he was twenty-three years old. Tommy's hustle was taking contracts, ten thousand dollars a buyer. His reasoning was that since he was already doing three life sentences—New York doesn't have capital punishment—if they give him another hundred years, so what? He's going to be there, so he might as well live sweet. These mob guys had the money to hire guys like Tommy. They had clout both inside and outside of prison, but they couldn't get out of jail, so they decided to live real good. They paid for what they wanted, but if a guard or an inmate wouldn't do something that they wanted, there was always a way to get them taken care of. And if it was a guard, of course these mob figures had connections on the outside.

And the guard had to go home, and that's where they would tag his ass.

Outside of the blatant power from the mob figures, each little community is broken down the same way. In the beginning while I was in Sing Sing, I still had a problem, because I looked black, but I'm Hispanic. I had been brought up in black Harlem, later moved to the Bronx, and then moved back down to Spanish Harlem. I had to just go back to my roots — to who I was. I'm Cuban. My mother was born here, but her parents were born in Cuba. So I had to cop to the Spanish gangs in prison. And I had to make that choice; there's no way I could have stayed in the middle, hanging out with both blacks and Hispanics. Nobody stands alone in prison. Otherwise you're very vulnerable. I had to become part of a gang even though I didn't want to, but basic prison survival dictates that you need strength. And basically when it comes down to getting shit done, you have to go to somebody.

Within the Spanish prison community, we had Carmen. He was a little guy but he was dangerous. And he was the person that we went to if we wanted something done. But Carmen had his own little thing — he liked little young guys, liked to fuck other little kids who came in. So he would be okay when it came to doing other things for us Spanish guys. But then he had his own little thing on the side. As long as he could fuck with them he didn't care if they were white, black, Spanish or whatever; this is what he wanted.

Sometimes a guy gets into trouble, and if he did something and antagonized somebody from another group, then that group came down on the Spanish group as a whole. So in order for you to be in line with any group in there, you have to understand that you have to deal with the bad part as well as the good part. You know, if our group is going strong at one time — if we have a lot of drugs or we have some inmates in there that are just some bad motherfuckers — then we sort of have the power. But as these guys get transferred out, or what have you, and the dynamics of the group change, then our power changes. So there were times where you could just walk around and say, "Yo man, that's one of our Latinos, leave him alone!" It wasn't really me the individual making a threat; it was the group as a whole. In other words, before they fuck with me, they would have to think about fucking with Carmen. And they didn't want to do that, so they left me alone.

EACH GANG HAD ITS OWN NETWORK or its own way of bringing in drugs. You had some guys who were stronger, who had a more steady or reliable pipeline to dealing in drugs. But there was a lot of independent drug rings. You couldn't get gigantic amounts in, but you could get dope in. But just like in the street, other guys don't like competition, so somebody might squeal on your old lady in the visiting room; they'd bust her right there. Or the guards would run up on you and you'd wonder where they got the word. These other gangs don't want that competition, so they would discourage you from bringing in your own drugs.

You can get drugs in a package. There are ways to doctor up packages, jars, cans, depending on what prison you're in and what they allowed to be sent into the package room. You can get drugs sent in through clothes. You have guys that work in the pharmacy, they steal. You have a business of women or men bringing drugs in or you may have a mule: somebody that is able to bring a big package of drugs right through the gate. That's either a CO or somebody that works in the penitentiary or a lawyer or somebody that has access to coming in and out. If not, the usual method is through a balloon. Most guys will get visits from their old lady, and they'll kiss them in the visiting room, and either swallow the balloon or put some grease on it and stick it in their ass. When you get back to your cell, you either regurgitate and throw it up or you take a shit. You stick your hand in the bowl and you take the balloon out and there's your drug. Most of these different ethnic groups have somebody who's involved in drugs. And they have their own system, their own way of bringing drugs into the joint.

Sometimes you can get guards to bring it in. A lot of guards I met in Sing Sing weren't opposed to bringing in dope and were doing it for other inmates for the money. They would set up an account on the outside. Most of the guys who had easy access to that system were big drug pushers who had gotten busted. They already had a network set up and they would make arrangements with the guard to pick up the money and the drugs and bring them in—and they did that.

Basically, you have the same types of drugs in prison that you have out on the street: heroin, cocaine, plenty of reefer. There were a lot of pills and acid and stuff like that, but that was mainly what the white boys liked to use—psychedelic drugs. So they would have their pipeline, their network, for bringing it in. Or sometimes during a visit, when the guards knew what was going on, they would not search certain inmates. Guys could walk in with a pocket full of goddamn drugs, you know, by paying off the guards. You can also make your own brew. You can get yeast, apples, fruit and stuff and you can ferment it in your cell. Alcohol is fairly easy to get, but all the heavy drugs you can also get.

Actually, we run the prison as far as getting things done. There's a prison subculture of gangs and little cliques who are in charge of different things. If I wanted a job assignment, I would go to an influential inmate who then would make whatever connections that were necessary with certain prison officials and give me my job assignment. I would have to pay for that some kind of way, but that's how it works. You might even have to pay for your cell assignment. When you come into prison, even if the COs assign you into a cell, if it happens to be in an area where there's a particular gang or group of guys functioning that don't want you there, then it doesn't make much difference where the prison assigns you. Staying in there would still be a hassle, because if the gang or whoever was in charge didn't want you in that cell they would just let you know that you aren't staying there. And they would make it very difficult for you to stay in that cell.

If you need something in prison, there are certain guys you can go to like the stashman. He had the stash. He held and traded everything from money to cigarettes. And certain influential inmates like the fixer worked arm in arm with the stashman. The fixer would get things done, like job reassignments and cell-block changes, and you'd have to pay, so he was actually hooked up with a stashman whose job was just to hold the stash and handle it. He made his deals on the side, but the fixer made more than the stash man. Or the stashman could trade stuff, turn things over. The price was always two for one; whatever it is, it's two for one.

SURVIVAL IS THE MAIN CHOICE that you have to make, and how you survive is up to you. The tension in prison is so thick you can cut it with a knife, and this is every day. Not once on Sunday and skip Monday and Tuesday; every single day you have to wake up and you have to be ready because you don't know what's going to happen. And you don't know who's going to start it and what direction it's going to come from. When I got up in Sing Sing I had it a little bit easy, because a fair number of COs that worked in my cell block used to buy dope from me when I was dealing out on the streets. You see, a brother of one of my customers was working at the time as a CO in Sing Sing, and he brought more COs to buy dope from me. So I had it pretty easy as far as discipline and some extra favors were concerned. The only difference between me and them is that I got caught and I had green and they had blue on. But they remembered me and I had a few privileges.

As I got further upstate, I got further away from the people that I knew, and I had to go into a different survival mode. Prison is not fun. There is no guarantee that you'll come out once you go in. You live in a powder keg. In any prison, if you have say a hundred guys, you have a hundred different attitudes. And these hundred different guys are thinking about a hundred different things, living in a cage, and are denied simple pleasures. The COs are sitting there and they fuck with you any way that they can. On any given day you don't know how you're going to respond to that pressure. And I mean this is constant pressure you're feeling. It's like pushing on your body. You have new guys coming in, you have new things happening, and prison is not the place to foster change, because getting used to a routine is your security. You know that you can make it because you know what the rules are. So as long as you go where you're supposed to go and do what you're supposed to do, you know that you'll survive. But when they change the routine, you get messed up. And because it's a dynamic situation with the constant changes in the inmate population, you don't really know where the new guys fit in, and that's another pressure. So you fall back into the suspicion and doubt all over again. And you do this many times. And a person was just not made to do this, to function this way, but you have to.

Every time you get transferred, every time you come to a new joint, you're going to get tested. You have to take an exam, you know; they have to know who you are, where you're at, what you're about. Even if your rep precedes you to an institution, when you get there physically, you have to re-inforce that reputation, because if not, you will lose it.

There are always informers — rats — in prison. I know two: one in Sing Sing and one in Clinton. They were going to kill the one in Sing Sing during a movie because he was inform-ing, not just on big shit, but little shit, too — petty shit. And the word got around because the guy got transferred from Comstock and his reputation followed him. A rat threatens the entire prison. So this is one of the few times we all got together. It was instant retaliation. But as we were coming into the movie, the guards smelled the violence too; they know when shit is going to go down. And they had an idea that something was going to happen. As a matter of fact, when we started going into the movie we noticed that there was double the usual number of guards. But before the inmates could get to him the guards took the rat out of the theater and locked him in protective custody.

The PC block is where you have not only your rats but also the real weak inmates — soft guys; they're not really fag-gots, but they're very liable to be if they put them away with the prison population. And some of your animals are kept in protective custody — guys who can't be put in the regular prison population. I mean, these guys aren't just antisocial; they don't give a fuck about anybody at any time. And some guys request PC, especially in the summertime. Prisons become pressure cookers due to the heat and the despair and the dynamics of prison life. Guys wake up every day just angry. And people that they normally wouldn't bother, or nor-mally even think about, they start to think about and bother. Some of these people are weaker, and some request PC.

Some older cons who have been down for a while are

respected because they know the system and they tend to tolerate things a little more. The more you go against the system the more you suffer. The older cons who have been there for a while tend to know the system and how to deal with it. And intelligence combined with strength is always admired. Sort of like a Solomon, you know, able to be an arbiter between arguments and be able to relate to administration, but yet be able to tell the administration to kiss his fucking ass and still get something done. Guys that know how to do time. You could do hard time or you could do easy time. These guys have a temperament that they don't push their machismo around all the time, but they don't back down from shit either. And every once in a while, they'll go off too. But on the whole, they seem to be pretty level-headed or pretty acclimated into their role of doing their time. And a lot of them won't reach out to you, but you'll see him from afar. Or you'll see him minding his own business, doing his thing, having things, you know, privileges, merchandise inside. And you say, how's this guy get to do all this shit, or how come he has all of that stuff? But he's earned that position; it's not given to him. You know, this guy sort of earns part of what he gets and takes some.

The social structure in prison is sort of like it is in the street. After a year or so of banging your head against the wall, and trying all other kinds of stuff, you begin to settle in a little. And you begin to realize what the structure of prison life is all about. So you try to find your spot and stay right there, you know, where everything is familiar. Prison life is about compromise. You have to compromise. I've seen a change from the James Cagney days when you had to be hard rocks; you know, him and Humphrey Bogart. Hard rocks don't really make it in prison anymore. You have to compromise, and you have to find some way to become comfortable with compromise. And you have to sort of define where that line ends.

You have to be able to relate to the guards and prison administration, but you also have to watch your ass so that you don't act in such a way to bring other inmates down on you. You have to find a way to do that. You're not going to hurt anybody but yourself if you play that hard rock shit.

Being in prison is not desirable and it's not easy. So you have to find a happy medium with that. And you still have an image to try to maintain and there's still a barrier between you and the COs—between you and the administration. You can't be sucking up to the COs and you can't be smacking a CO, or something like that, because you're going to end up doing more time. You have to think about it: is it worth it? So usually, after you've been down for a while, these are the things that you start to think about, so this is how you find these little compromises.

In all the state joints I've been in, there are always certain understood rules among inmates. Like, you don't walk into another inmate's cell. You don't violate that door space. That's automatic ass whipping. You don't fuck with another inmate's food. You don't—basically it's crazy, but you don't steal from one another. A lot of times you'll lock out of your cell and you can't just close the door and lock your stuff in there. So anybody that does do that is subject to an ass whipping.

THE DEPARTMENT OF CORRECTIONAL SERVICES only supplies you with certain things: a towel, a toothbrush, that hardass lye soap. If you want other things—candy, cigarettes, things like that—you have to buy it from the commissary. I didn't have any family or anybody sending me money, so I had to develop a hustle for myself while I was inside. Eventually, I got to be what's called a jailhouse lawyer. I used to fight inmates' cases, do appeals for them and other things, and the system doesn't like that. They frown on that, because it's sort of like you're organizing; you're letting the inmates know their rights. I know a lot of people don't like to hear about it, but inmates have rights, too, and a lot of times the administration conveniently forgets that. And they don't give inmates certain things that by law they're supposed to have. I would find out, and I would put it on paper, and file a legal motion for the guy. I'd get paid anything from a couple of cartons of cigarettes to a watch, a ring, a gold chain, cash money, extra food, or reefer, which I in turn resold.

I had a GED high school diploma, and I could read and follow directions. Words and writing never bothered me; as a matter of fact, I like to write and read, so being able to do it for profit—you know, one thing led to another. When I was on Rikers Island I did a lot of writing, Spanish and English, and I wrote a lot of poetry and things. And I used to help this other guy who was fighting an appeal from a conviction. He had gotten a murder conviction and he was doing a lot of legal work, and he had gotten it appealed and was getting another trial. And he and I became good buddies, and I sort of got the idea from him. So by the time I got into the state system, I more or less figured out how I was going to do my hustling. And it was by getting access to a law library. It was tedious, there was a lot of reading and a lot of work, but I had a lot of time.

From the perspective of the administration, I was a troublemaker, and nobody wants troublemakers in their prison. After I got to Clinton they sent me to Attica. The state system doesn't like jailhouse lawyers. They want to keep guys in there and don't want any problems. So, consequently, I was transferred around to a lot of prisons. They come knocking on your cell, maybe four or five o'clock in the morning, tell you to pack your shit—you're leaving in five minutes. That's it. So I got to the point where I would pack light, because I never knew when I was leaving an institution.

PRISONS ARE FOR PUNISHMENT. PRISON as a rehabilitative apparatus does not work. What prison does right now is it takes the offender off the street and away from society; and at this point, that's all society is interested in doing. They're not interested in rehabilitation, correction or anything else. The prisons are too overcrowded at this point for that to happen even if they wanted it to happen. So what we're caught up in right now is warehousing. And what they want to do is build more warehouses. It's hard to get rehabilitated in a prison setting. Prisons just don't function that way. The rules that you use to survive in prison don't work out here. The rules that you live by out here, don't work in prison. There has to be a transition. But society seems to want to apply all that money towards building more warehouses as opposed to addressing the social problems and the transition that would be needed to "rehabilitate" these inmates. In effect what they're doing is just propagating this criminal behavior and just waiting for this inmate to strike again so they can fill up some more space and lock him back up.

When you step out of prison you're an ex-convict, and that's a tag that you have to wear for the rest of your life. There are certain rights that you have to wait to get back: the right to vote, to get a passport, and stuff like that. There are certain jobs that you're barred from getting because you're an ex-offender. And part of it is that you really don't hook back up into the proper network. You could walk out of prison and go home, I mean, very repentant of your crime and want to do something to try to get your life back together. But then those stepping stones are closed off to you simply because you're an ex-convict. So you have to sort of try a little extra harder and do things maybe in a roundabout way and your discipline has to be very, very strong. But for just an ordinary person it's hard. When he goes back to his family, it's usually a family that's broken or a dysfunctional family. You're not much into going to church. Even if you take some college courses in prison, there are still certain occupations that are closed off. So you spend a lot of time maybe getting training in electronics or something and then come out and find out you can't get a job in electronics. What do you do?

I went to Canton Tech College in New York for an interview to see if I could apply to go to school there. And they told me, basically, they would be scared to death to have me on campus at this time. They wanted me to come back out in the community and work and do the right thing for a year and then reapply in 1991. So when I walked out, I wanted to tell them to kiss my black ass, but what I told them was thank you very much for the consideration that you gave to my applying to school. But then I thought about it. If I come out of prison and can't get a job because I'm an ex-convict and I don't have any skills; and if I can't go to school to get the skills, what the fuck am I supposed to do? Most ordinary guys will simply give up.

Prison doesn't deter people from committing crimes or deter inmates when they get out. Even the death penalty is not going to deter anybody, because all you have to do is say it's not going to happen to you, or you're not going to get caught, and then you go ahead and do what you have to do. Prison didn't stop me from doing anything—all the dope, the robberies, the burglaries. The dread of going to prison didn't mean anything. I thought about it, but I really didn't give a shit. Even when I was in county jail, none of those threats worked.

It wasn't until I got to a minimum-security prison that anybody gave me any encouragement, any hope. At that time, I was still doing law work, but I was the editor of the newspaper. And my boss was the head librarian. She was an idealist—she saw good in everybody—and she was very naive even though she worked in a prison. But she was about the only one that showed any interest in me. For everybody else, even the counselors, you'd just be a number, just a number. *Numero Uno* was the name of the newspaper. It was sort of like a self-esteem type of thing, I guess, for the inmates being in there. We would write articles about dances and holidays, and I started putting crossword puzzles in the paper and printing articles and poetry from some of the inmates; you know, giving them something to do, something to take pride in.

My boss saw that I was pretty good with words, and I wouldn't have that much of a problem putting it on paper. A lot of people can talk nice, but they're scared to write it down on paper. She saw that I didn't have that type of fear. And that I could use words and I knew what words were; I just didn't sling them around. And she wanted to encourage that in me, and she did. And when the guy that was origi-nally the editor got released on parole, I became editor.

9

C H A P T E R

PLAYING WITH FIRE

I MET JOAN WHEN I WAS IN THE minimum joint upstate and she was a nurse. I had an umbilical hernia problem, which I still have. I was getting migraine headaches also at the time, so I was going to the medical building quite a lot. And being the player that I am, I picked up certain vibes. But she's married, and her husband is a pillar of the community. Being in prison, I played with the fantasy for a while. And one day I decided to see if what I was thinking was what she was thinking because I started to get certain signs. But I was scared to respond to them because she's white and works in the prison. I'm black and I'm an inmate. And there is no middle line. And there is no acceptance for that type of relationship. It could have gotten me killed. The least that they would have done would be to whip my ass, send me back to a maximum joint, and add more time to my sentence. I mean, this has been done before. I'm not that naive. But I had to find out.

So one day I concocted some bullshit story, and I ended up in the medical building. And I guess she was going along the same lines as I was. There was nobody else in the medical building. She was sitting down behind a desk, and then I said something about it's time to leave, and she said to wait a minute. She got up and she walked me to the door and we were kind of close. So I took a chance. I kissed her and she kissed me, and we started a relationship from there. And it was difficult for me. I didn't really understand what the dynamics behind our whole relationship were, and what she was looking for and everything else. In the beginning, I don't think I was in love with her, but I would have treated her very respectfully and kindly and everything else because of what she had shown me. And especially being in prison and a long way from home.

I found out later that her husband abuses her and she has three kids. And that she had never been in an extra-marital affair before. After she was married, she never had another man besides her husband. So I didn't really know where I fit into all of that. All I knew was I had somebody that cared about me and I was willing to care back; to show as much care and concern, appreciation and feeling that she was willing to show me. Joan's rich. She's well off. She didn't have to work, but she worked. After a while I began to see that I was just filling a gap in her life. She's got everything else a woman can ask for: a home, kids, family, job, money. But her husband—I guess there's a female need that he just wasn't fulfilling.

Our relationship in prison went on for six or seven months. And I was scared to death every time we had sex in the medical building. At times I was so scared, I even had trouble getting a hard-on. We'd get together during lunch-time because the medical building is empty between twelve and one when the inmates are eating. You see, they ran that prison very sloppily, even the medical building. And because the COs have to eat, there would be no one in there. There are specific times for a medical call-out: nine in the morning to twelve noon and one to three in the afternoon, unless there was a special reason and the nurse had to call you over there. You couldn't go over on your own. So Joan used to call me out once in a while. And I would go over to the medical building until they got hip to what was happening. Then they kept a guard there all the time. But Joan created a very dangerous environment for me, because she wasn't affected by the shit I was. She didn't have to worry about her job. She just thought that they weren't going to fire her from her job and that we could just carry on like it's our right. And I kept trying to explain it to her: it isn't our right.

After a while, I had a deputy superintendent on my ass, I had the warden on my ass, I had the other COs on my ass, I had the inmates on my ass because of what I'm doing. And there are no secrets in prison. I had to fight other inmates who wanted to use me to get to her—for money, gifts, drugs, and everything else. I was the only one having a female while in prison. And everybody knew it. Joan would buy me gold, she would buy me watches. And a lot of guys were jealous, so I had to keep peace with them, I had to keep peace with the administration, and I had to keep Joan away from me. In the beginning it was fun, it was okay. When we had sex, I was still scared half to death, because that's all I needed to do was to get caught fucking a white woman inside a penitentiary. All she had to do is scream rape. Even if she didn't, they would.

I was always scared. But for her it was an attraction. I was the editor of the newspaper, and my office was in the administration building. The nurse would have to come by every morning to give call-outs to guys that they needed to see for medical reasons the next day. And Joan used to come by my office all the time. And it finally got to the point where I told her it was getting too hot, and "When you come in this building from now on, you go do what you have to do and get the hell out. Don't come by my office." But she's tiptoeing through the tulips, man. She'd come in and she'd sit down in the office, and she'd talk to the COs and other guys in there as if everything was all right. And I'm saying, "Joan, it's not all right." And she says, "Yes it is." And I'm telling her, "Get the hell out of here! You're going to get me killed!" But, you know, this is her dream come true and she can't see why other people won't accept what's going on.

The administration told me outright: leave Joan alone. But because I was the editor of the newspaper and I was also knowledgeable about law—and because I wasn't just an ass-hole from New York that they could threaten like that—they had to deal with me in a different way. They weren't used to dealing with Johns like me. They're used to saying something and having inmates jump. Or making a threat and scaring the shit out of them. I'm not like that, I'll take them to the wall. So they tried to mess with me legally. And I had to keep them off of me.

They couldn't actually prove the physical part of our relationship, but Joan and I were getting real sloppy. I mean, all the stuff that she bought for me, she would bring it right in. I got watches and rings that did not come into the package room. There's no number or anything on it. Nor is there any slip saying that this gold and jewelry came in through the package room. So legally, I'm in violation. That's contraband. I never asked her to bring drugs, but she would have if I asked. I knew at that time I was doing everything else and getting away with it and playing a game. All I needed to do was get caught with some drugs, man, that's it. I used to have Joan bring in stuff I ordered, like caviar, crab legs, suede jackets and lots of other stuff. I stopped shopping in the commissary once I got going with Joan. I would make her shop in the grocery stores outside and bring my stuff in. She'd call me out around twelve o'clock noon. I'd come to the medical building and pick up my packages and take them back to my cell block. Security there is real sloppy. Joan would bring my stuff in and they would watch me leave the medical building with two bags full of food and God knows what else in there. And I'd go back to my cell and lock it in.

The COs in this prison were weak. A lot of them had been trying to screw Joan for years. And once they saw and knew what she was doing, they would try and talk to her outside the prison. But she was married and her husband used to own a line of drugstores in the area. And this prison used to have a contract where they bought all their pharmaceuticals from his drug stores. Her husband is a Republican and he's politically active. So they were scared to fuck with her because that would mean fucking with him, and he could take their jobs, you know. One of the COs was trying to screw Joan for a long time. And every chance he got he would try to mess with me. But I would make sure that I just wasn't under his area of domain.

It finally just got to the point where it was too much for me to deal with because Brown, a deputy superintendent, was after me. They used to shake down my cell all the time, but I had built up a rep with some of the COs and I had my crew of COs that I could relate to. And they saw what was happening. And they knew me as a person, and they didn't really care what I was doing. And I wasn't doing anything illegal. I was trying to get my shit together. That's how they accepted it. So whenever there was a shakedown, I wouldn't even know about it, but I would have one of the COs in the block go with the sergeant and this deputy superintendent. Brown is a complete asshole. He thinks he's God and he thinks he runs the prison. And he thinks there's nothing that goes on in prison that he doesn't know about and that he can't control. Until I came along. I just fucked that all up.

They've been running this prison this way for years and years. The wardens have changed, but Brown has always been there. So Brown was shaking me down. He came with the sergeant to my cell, and some of the COs that I was friendly with would tell me that somebody's trying to put drugs in my cell. But they'd say, "Don't worry about it, because I'm not going to sign the contraband report. And if I don't sign the report the rest of them can't sign it either." So Brown got kind of frustrated that way.

One day, I decided to interview him for an article for the newspaper. I was talking to him up on the third floor. And I had my gold watch and gold chain on. Brown is a little shorter than me, and he's looking right at the gold. So I knew once I left Brown what was up. He didn't do anything then, he was cool. I went down to my office and I saw my man, Benito, coming in. And I said, "Benito, do me a favor. Take this gold and put it on. Brown is going to bust me before I walk out the building. But I have to let you know it's hot. Brown knows it's mine." He said, "Man, don't worry about it." And Benito was an old timer, so he was glad to do it. Sure enough, walking out the building, six minutes later, Brown's got all the COs there, and he walks up to me and he just looks. He backed away from me. He knew. The gold was gone. I haven't got it. What was he going to do—bust me for contraband? I haven't got any contraband.

I sort of tried to keep everything I did on a low profile. I didn't just run around blatantly doing shit all the time. But

I did enough to get my way when I had, you know, room to get my way. And then I would back up a little bit. The lady that was my boss for the newspaper used to get scared for me a lot. And she'd say, "Ronald, why do you keep doing this? You know, something's going to happen to you." And I would tell her, "What are they going to do to me, lock me up? I'm locked up now. I don't care. Anything is better than what's happening to me right now."

About six months before the end of my sentence, I applied to the temporary release committee to be allowed to go on work release to look for a job, because I had decided to relocate in Albany when my time was up. But they refused my request. So they sent me down to Fulton Work Release in the Bronx. They locked me up there for seven days of solitary, and then they sent me back to the upstate joint, which is unheard of. Once you leave the prison, you never go back to the same institution. They did not have the legal right to send me down to a place I did not want to go to. Inmates have the right to ask for relocation, not to be sent back to the original place of the arrest. And I knew this. And they knew it. So they tried to shove me out of the Albany area. But I sure stopped that shit, and I got back up there. But then I had to walk a chalk line for the remaining time I was there. I applied for temporary work release again, but that faggot ass, Smith, used to run the temporary release committee. And he was God in his little division. So I asked him one day, "Why aren't you going to give me work release?" He said, "The hell with you, man, we aren't giving you anything."

So I went to the law books. And I drew up a motion to show cause based on Article 76. In other words, tell me legally why you're not giving me what I'm asking for, which I'm legally within my rights as an inmate to have. But in essence what it also does is it puts the issue in front of a federal judge. So actually you're going above their heads. I asked Smith a couple of times. As a matter of fact, I went through the Inmate Grievance Committee, I went to the warden, I went to the deputy in charge of security, which for me was just more ammunition for my lawsuit. I would write a request stating my situation and why I think that I qualify for this and that, and Smith would send it back

through the mail. You know, you sent a written request—
they call them bombs—for something. So you drop a bomb.
You put it in one of the wooden boxes in the administration
building and it's taken by a clerk to whomever it's addressed.

So Smith thought he was slick. He takes my bomb and
sends it through the US mail. I get a response to my request
like three days later: "We're not giving you work release. Don't
ask for it anymore." And he wrote this down. That was Exhibit
A. I made him put everything on paper. Everything. I went
to the Inmate Grievance Committee. I went to the warden.
I made him write his statement on paper. And the day before
I filed this motion 76, I mailed out two copies by certified
mail. Both Commissioner Coughlin and the State Director
of Temporary Release for all the prisons in the State of New
York had their copies two days before I dropped the article
inside the prison. I got it postaged through the mail room
in the prison. And they didn't know what the hell I was doing.
I finally did get my temporary release—on paper. But they
only let me out twice a week to go look for a job.

Meanwhile, Joan had locked onto a dream—this fantasy
life—of me and her. The fact that she was married, had kids,
was planted in the community, and everything else seemed
to slip her mind. By this time, Joan had gotten really blatant. She didn't care about the administration doing anything
because as far as she was concerned they wouldn't touch her.
She would keep coming by the office until they started to
station a CO right outside in front of my office just to bar
her from coming in. One New Year's, Joan called the cell
block and the only thing that saved me was the CO that was
on, Macky, who's a black guy, and he knew me. So we were
all right. The dumb bitch calls the cell block at seven o'clock
in the morning. Macky wakes me up to bring me to the telephone for her to wish me a Happy New Year's. I said, "Joan,
are you crazy? If this was another CO, I'd be packing my shit
up to go to the max joint right now."

"Oh, baby, but I just wanted to . . ."

I said, "No!" Then I had to explain the dynamics to her.
I said, "Joan, you don't seem to understand what's going on.
Right now, they're trying to discourage what you're doing.
They're going to protect you because you're white. It's not

your fault. It's my fault. We are weak-minded and we just happen to be caught up in this inmate game. They'll try to protect you, but you've already passed that stage. So now what they might try to do is transfer you somewhere to forcibly get you away from the situation. But you've gone past that too. So the only other option that's open to them is to write you off along with me. And by doing that they'll fire you but they will hang my black ass. Don't you understand that?"

"But honey, it's all right because I love you."

I said, "Get the fuck away from me! Don't come by my office. Don't do anything!" She didn't listen. So they fired me from my job in the newspaper office.

When I applied for parole I was denied the first time and told to come back six months later because my release at this time would be incompatible with the welfare and well-being of society. The second time they granted my parole, but they would not release me to Albany unless I had a place to go. And I had to do all this juggling from inside the prison. But I finally did it, because one of the guys that I used to know in Albany, a black bus driver, he and I used to talk. And his mother just happened to have a private house and she was willing to give me a room, at least to start out. So I made Joan give her something like five hundred dollars for the first two months or whatever, because I knew the money would make it easier for her to put me up.

So I came back with an address. And the administration was astounded that I managed to take care of all of this, which they knew I couldn't take care of because they wouldn't let me out to take care of it. And where was I getting this money from? And then they tell me I have to have 250 dollars in my inmate account, an address, and a job. But I got around that. I got the promise of at least a job interview on paper and I had 250 dollars in my account. They wanted to know where this money was coming from. I said, "Man, screw that. You told me to have it in the account—I have it in the account." They said, "No, we have a new rule now. You have to have 450 dollars." I said, "Check it tomorrow" and I told Joan, "Put 250 more dollars in my account, and bring me the receipt." You know, it went up to five hundred dollars. I had that five hundred dollars to get out of prison. I had it. I said, "How are you going to stop me now?" So reluctantly they discharged me.

But to be honest, they had cut me down to no activity in the prison. None. I couldn't work, I couldn't use the library. I had no recreation. And my nerves started to rattle me. I couldn't afford to get a ticket even for spitting on the ground. A ticket is what they give you for an infraction in prison. And then you have to go before a disciplinary committee. It was kind of hard to walk a straight line, because I had to deal with that shit from the inmates and the pressure from the administration. And I did that for about two months. And I couldn't take it any more. Finally, you know, guys were teasing me and fucking with me and disrespecting me. And I'm not answering back to that. The prison is not the place for you to do that. But I'm trying to walk this straight line so I can get the hell out of here. You know, it didn't matter to me backing down on this or that. Because I knew I was still a man. But it finally got to me. And one Monday night, I said, "The hell with it. When I wake up in the morning the first person to fuck with me, I don't care who it is—a guard, an inmate—I'm taking him out." I'm not kidding. I didn't give a fuck. They had jerked me around on my parole. I had met all the parole conditions, and I was still in prison.

So when I woke up in the morning, I just didn't care. The CO came to my door and he said, "Look, your papers came through. Get dressed. You're leaving." That's the only thing that saved me, because I was determined that even if somebody didn't bother me, I was going to mess with somebody. I had been holding this in too long. And I'm thinking about all those motherfuckers that disrespected me and all this other shit, but I wasn't backing down anymore. Yo, man, I was going to do some damage. And they would have locked me up for another year, and added more time to my sentence. And then when I went to the parole board, they would have said, "Well, you've been doing this, so we're going to give you some more time." But I didn't care, man.

After I got out of prison I continued to see Joan. She had a lot of money and I used it. I bought clothes, an apartment. As long as I found time to have physical relations with Joan, everything was all right. She had a schedule and she's a busy woman. And as long as I found time to fit into that schedule and satisfy her physically, everything was cool. Her husband knew about our relationship. But I kept the relationship away from him and his house. And in my mind he's the type of man that was screwing some other broad in one of his drugstores. I mean, he stopped being with Joan a long time ago. And I guess he just felt far removed from that. As long as he didn't have to save face, I guess he just didn't give a damn.

If Joan and I were seen together that would have been grounds for revoking my parole and locking me back up. It was all fantasy: her family would accept me coming into their lives and everything would be hunky dory. And I had a hard time with this, and it was stressing me out, too. Trying to maintain my sense of reality and just being able to serve Joan and have her financially take care of me. I just had to be available when she wanted me to be available. And I really didn't like that idea. So I fought against it. And then she would pull the strings here and pull the strings there. Yet, to this day, she's still talking love shit. These dynamics have always been the same, I guess. I just didn't understand them in the beginning. I understand them now. I don't know whether she's doing this on purpose or she doesn't know any better or whatever. At this point, it doesn't make any difference. If you leave it up to Joan, she just wants to fuck all the time. As long as she could come home and come to bed with me and I'm ready to take her, then everything is fine. But the fact that I have my own desires and needs and wants—I mean, that just doesn't come into the picture. I seriously doubt if we will ever get together.

I had decided to relocate to Albany. I wanted to relocate since I had no family or place or anything else to go back to in New York. So I figured, hell, if I can live in New York, I could live anywhere else in the world. So I decided to start my life anew in Albany. I put in for work release and eventually after I dropped the court order, I got work release in Albany. But my parole officer, Bill Barlow, had the attitude that I was going to mess up, and he was going to wait until I messed up and lock me back up. The first day I went to his office, he strip-searched me. He thought I was foolish enough to come into his office, one hour out of prison, with a weapon or drugs or something else. Plus he wanted to show me he was the boss, he was God, he was the man, what he said goes. Obviously, he didn't know who I was. So I ended up spending the first year and a half on parole just staying out of situations that could be roughly misconstrued as me being in trouble.

It took me about eight months to find a job. Every time you fill out a job application, those applications have a box and it says, have you ever been convicted of a crime? If you say no, and they decide to investigate, that's grounds for firing you. If you say yes—through my experience—that's grounds for not hiring you. And since Albany is a political town and you had to have either a college degree or know someone to get a state job, it was very difficult to get a decent job. Through the parole office, I finally got a job working in a goddamn factory on Railroad Avenue taking apart old car alternators with a hammer, getting my fingers all torn up for minimum wage, dealing with all kinds of chemicals and rust. I did that for about a week and a half, and I quit. Most of the jobs the parole officer helps you get are shit work, donkey work—you know, idiot work, manual labor. And I thought I was above that kind of work, and I was, and I am. So I told the boss after a week and a half, "Yo man, I'm not coming in tomorrow or anymore, I quit."

By this time, I had gotten Barlow, my PO, to back off me. I had got reluctant respect from him, because he ran up on me a couple of times, and I ran him back off me. He had me reporting once a week, every damn week. When I came to report, I was clean, decent, you know; and at this time I wasn't getting in trouble with drugs or alcohol or anything else, so he really had nothing that he could come down on me about. And I didn't fit the regular stereotype of the guys that he was used to dealing with. In fact, I felt out of place as soon as I walked in the parole office. Those other guys are dressed like bums, haven't got any jobs, they're getting high.

I couldn't find a decent job in Albany, so I decided to go to school. I enrolled in Russell Sage Junior College of Albany, but didn't finish the semester.

10

TURNING IT AROUND

THE FIRST TIME I ENTERED A
drug rehab program was in 1969. My mother took me. The
second time, I was in the same drug rehab in 1971. I had
relapsed and I had gotten arrested for possession of dope,
works, and stolen property; and I had a lot of outstanding
warrants on me. One of the cops who arrested me suggested
that if I entered a program they'd drop the charges against
me. So I contacted James Allen, the director of the Addicts
Rehabilitation Center (ARC), and entered a therapeutic community in Patterson, New Jersey. I stayed in the program for
about thirteen months.

ARC was a live-in therapeutic community and there was
no medication at all. When I first came into the program I
was sick for a couple of weeks because of withdrawal from
the drugs. The program gradually starts you off in what's
called therapy. Every day I had to go through a therapy ses-
sion, which would last anywhere from one to two hours, two
or three times a day.

I resisted in the beginning because I didn't want to stop
shooting dope. I really didn't want to live without getting
high. And I thought this program and everything else about
giving up dope was all bullshit. As for therapy being the
answer, I didn't take to that until I was in the program for

163

like six months. I fought it every step of the way. But James Allen had a belief that just because drugs are out there, you don't have to use them. And he himself was a recovering addict, so he knew how to deal with other dope fiends, because we're full of a lot of games. My life revolves around games. That's how we make our money, by games.

I thought that I was sharp, but I was in a therapeutic center with other dope fiends from the middle of Harlem. And I think those are the slickest dope fiends in the world. They knew every game—backwards, forwards, up, down, sideways. In the beginning we're all like that. I think it's a survival mechanism; we just don't want to give up those games. And I think that's what the months and months of concentrated therapy does. Getting away from narcotics is not just a physical game; it's a mental game. You have to readjust all over again, and you have to learn how to live and be motivated to want to live drug-free. Our lives have revolved around drugs so much that drugs were the center point of our being. Without drugs I really didn't have any motivation to live. I didn't think that I could live without getting high.

In the beginning, the friends that I had were all full of shit just like I was. They were all ducking and dodging one way or another. But part of the therapy is that it's reality therapy: you deal with real situations, and if you're talking about a bunch of bullshit somebody will call you up on it. They'd use aggressive confrontational techniques which they called marathon sessions. When I first came into the program I was a participant, but then I became the object of a lot of these marathon sessions. And I would sit in a chair in a room with maybe ten to fifteen other residents and they would just go after me, because I would be trying to explain a point, or trying to say something, when really I was in denial stage. And these people who are my peers—drug addicts—also are people who have more or less time than me in the program. But since I was the object, I was the one that they'd choose to take their frustrations out on. And I had to learn how to deal with this. I mean, we did everything but physical violence. It was rough.

There are different levels of job responsibility in the therapeutic community, and you gradually worked your way through three phases on the way to reentry. Reentry is when you're ready to look for a job or training or something and reenter back into society. During the last couple of months of therapy, I moved to the Addicts Rehabilitation Center located in Manhattan on 23rd Street between 7th and 8th Avenues. And it was at this point that the director of the program, James Allen, used to take me and another resident with him on speaking engagements to talk to other groups about drug problems. Allen is a very dynamic individual. I used to think of him as the king of bullshit, because you couldn't bullshit him. And I eventually found that his strength came from his honesty and his truth. And he would state simple points. I think Allen started to see something in me that I didn't see in myself, because eventually he started giving me assignments to take another resident with me to fulfill his speaking engagements.

During the time I was involved in these engagements, I also graduated from the program, because I had completed my time there. My first position, which Allen was instrumental in getting for me, was as an awareness counselor. I worked for the Board of Education and my office was located in PS 125. I gave talks on drugs and my specific job was to bring awareness of drugs into the school system. I had my own staff there and I was also part of a larger organization. The name of the program was SASP, Save the Addicted Student Population.

After I left Allen and went to work for the Board of Education, I began to meet a lot of people. I became a little more comfortable in the fact that I could live a drug-free life and my self-esteem rose. This was hard for me to envision, it was hard for me to take, and it was hard for me to think about, because I was basically still in the same environment. At this time I was living in the South Bronx, but I was going back and forth to work in Manhattan on 123rd Street and Amsterdam Avenue.

FROM ABOUT 1974 TO 1979 I was clean most of the time, and most of the jobs I had during this period were geared to the counseling profession. I was basically a counselor for ex-offenders. And at the time, they were not called recovering addicts, they were called ex-dope fiends. I found out that I had an affinity towards that type of work and I liked it. And I knew what I was talking about. So I gravitated towards those types of jobs. Also, I entered a few colleges. I always started, but I never finished a full semester in any of them. Up until this point, I never really completed anything in my life. I always started a million projects and then I'd get impatient with them. I was going to school, but I was also working, and I had a kind of active social life. I attended Fordham University, Hostos Community College, and Harper College in SUNY Binghamton. And when I got out of the Job Corps in 1967, I went to Northeastern University in Boston for a while. I never earned a full semester of credits at any of these schools.

Actually, it was a dry period, as opposed to really recovering. I was basically abstinent, because I had started to discover a new drug-free world. I was starting to do some of the things that I was doing before, but I wasn't getting high. In recovery, you learn that people, places, and things are something that you have to change. I didn't do that. I went back to some of the same old guys I was hanging out with except I wasn't shooting dope. And pretty soon I started selling dope again, did a stickup or two, but mainly drug dealing, because I found it easier to deal drugs than to do stickups. When I had left Allen's program but was still surrounded by rehabilitation—you know, going back to the house and talking to James Allen and everything—I managed to keep my head balanced. I knew where I was going, and I knew how I was going to get there. But when I got away from Allen, I got into myself, and I sort of figured as long as I stayed away from shooting dope, I would be okay, which turned out not to be the case. The further I got away from the program, the further I got away from the things that I really needed in order to really put my foot down firm and get a solid foundation.

The guys I was hanging around with were also dealing or shooting dope and into street crimes. I enjoyed the fact that I could walk around clean, had a lot of money, and didn't have to worry about the cops looking for me. So when the cops came around they were looking for one of those other guys. And here I was doing some of the same shit. I even worked for the criminal justice agency in Bronx Central Booking for a couple of months, but I got tired of that job, too.

After a while I couldn't go back to Allen, because I knew he was the only one in the world that could see through the game I was playing again. So I stayed away from him. Consequently, I stayed away from the one person who could have saved me, because everybody else I could bullshit, and bullshit them well.

I had gotten married; I think it was in 1972. I was legally married for about two years, but we only lived together for about four or five months and then separated. We never really had a life. I met Lucille in the ARC program, and I did what you're not supposed to do: I got involved with a girl in the program—an ex-dope fiend—coming through rehab. And I figured that we would run away and live a charmed life but that's bullshit. When we married, Lucille was on welfare, I was selling dope and reefer, so we had money, and I had a job working for YSA, the Youth Services Agency. We were in charge of summer programs—entertainment programs—for the kids. We would go to the neighborhoods and set up a block party, bands, public swimming pools, circuses—youth activities for the summertime.

I got divorced from Lucille and for about four or five months I began sniffing dope a little bit again. Then I entered a methadone program. During the time my divorce was in the courts I had met Lois—Lourdes in Spanish—and we had a daughter, Kimberly, who was born in 1976. We lived together but never got legally married. When I met Lois, who is Puerto Rican, I decided to clean up. That's about the time I started at Hostos Community College, and I decided to detox from the methadone program. I had decided that Kimberly's mother was worth cleaning up my act. And I wanted to be drug-free and get my life together. I thought methadone was the way out, but it really wasn't, because the only thing I wasn't doing was shooting dope. My mentality was still the same. And the time that I was on the meth program, I was shooting cocaine.

In the methadone program, I'd pick up my medication

at 8:00 in the morning, because if I got there at 8:30 I had to crawl up the stairs to get my medication. That methadone started to withdraw from my body and you get sick, violently sick from not having the drug in your system. Methadone is a twenty-four hour medication. With methadone in your system, you can't feel heroin. If you inject heroin off of methadone, you're liable to overdose. So what methadone does is negate the feeling that you would get from heroin. It substitutes for the heroin. But it doesn't do anything for your mind, which is what getting away from all this shit is about. You can detox the chemical out of your system for three days or two weeks, but what are you going to do with your mind? What are you going to do with your motivation? This is what therapy is all about. This is what recovery is all about. You know, you just can't put down the drug and expect to start living drug-free. Methadone is sup-posed to take care of all this. The methadone program was set up for you to have counselors and get jobs and all that, which is bullshit, because nobody wants anybody that's on methadone. It's like coming out with an ex-offender back-ground. Once they find out you're on methadone, they don't want you working. And rightly so, because while you're on methadone it's just like you're on dope. Your reflexes slow down. Guys fall asleep in machine shops and cut up their body parts, or have accidents.

And guys I knew still committed crimes while on the methadone program. The methadone took care of two things: you weren't sick from the withdrawal of heroin and you had a lot of time on your hands, because you didn't have to go out there and stick people up to get the money to buy the dope. But you still had the game in your head. I was bored. What the hell am I going to do now? What am I going to do with my day? How am I going to spend my day? I have all this time and I'm on welfare. The counseling was a joke. I mean, you're rocking off that methadone, so when you sit in your counselor's office and he's talking, you say, "Yeah, yeah, okay. I'll go here, I'll go there." But the only thing you did was what the welfare people told you to do so that they could keep sending you that money and keep paying for your methadone. Only a very few people that I know lead a productive life holding down a legitimate job while on methadone. Methadone tears you down, it takes its toll. I was in the program three years and left.

I was going to Hostos Community College on government loans and Pell grants and there was no way that I could study and be on the program, because I had to be at that methadone program every day to pick up that medication. And I was still playing mental games with myself. I really didn't have a grip on the way I was going. And I had already isolated myself from the people that were meaningful or that could have helped. I bullshitted them so well they thought I was doing really great, but I wasn't.

I would stay in a school for a little while, but then it became boring. Looking back at it now, I was never really totally motivated. I couldn't see where school fit into what I was doing. School was just something else to do. It was the right thing to do. But I didn't have any solid motivation towards going to school. I used to go to class and take exams but I didn't study at all. I met a lot of broads and I met some more people so I could play some new games. School was just something that I knew I should do, but I never treated it with the respect that I do now. Then I was still living one day at a time, and I was still living a lot of dreams. I was never really grounded, you know, I was like fluttering, flying around. So except for the meth, I was staying clean, but I was still selling dope and still hanging around with the same guys. I was still going to the same places. The only thing I wasn't doing was getting high. At that point in my life, I still had temptations — cravings for dope — but I had said in my mind: I'm not going to do that, and I didn't for quite a while.

AFTER I WAS RELEASED FROM PRISON for the stickup of the numbers bankers in 1984, I got paroled to Albany. I had a white redneck parole officer whose attitude was that I was a slick motherfucker from New York, and since he couldn't get my game right away, he was going to play me until he found out what my game was and then he was going to lock me back up. And this was the basis for our relationship. When I got off parole, I had been living in Albany for three years, but

I hadn't built up a support network for myself. And I guess I had come out of prison with some life issues that I never really addressed or dealt with. I found myself alone. So I hung onto that for a while until all of it came to a head again. I found my only release was to get involved in drugs again.

I had isolated myself from people. I had tried to set goals and things in my mind, but again, looking back on it retrospectively, I had isolated myself from everything. I had no one that I could confide in. No one that I could talk to. I didn't have positive people that I could even go hang out with. I knew them, but only in a peripheral way. You know, I never let anybody close to me. Intermittently I had some legitimate jobs after I came out of prison but they would get to the point where I would become frustrated, because I couldn't see where this job was going to lead. And I really didn't know where I wanted to go. And I had no idea how I was going to get there. By 1985, I was getting high again. Then I stopped for a little while and in 1988 I started heavy again.

I'm a dope fiend: the only type of drugs I like is dope—heroin. I don't mess with anything else. I don't like alcohol. If I'm going to use narcotics, I'm going straight to heroin. In Albany, I sort of had to retrain my system to shoot dope maybe once or twice a day, because dope is really expensive there. Real expensive. Eventually, I got into driving down to New York City and buying my own dope at New York City prices. And then to make my money back, I would sell dope in Albany. So it got to the point where I was constantly driving back and forth from New York to Albany.

I had good dope, and once I let people know I had good dope, I had customers. The problem with that is that Albany is really not a dope hustler's place to be. The people there are really not skilled in the art of what real street life is all about. There are a lot of rats. Albany's a petty town—there's a lot of pettiness, especially in the street people. So I not only had to watch out for the cops, I had to watch out for the people I sold the drugs to. They'd turn me in in a minute.

I had known all along that my heart really wasn't into shooting dope again. I didn't turn to drugs this time to fill the drug need that I had. It was more or less to fill the gaps that were in my life. And I just didn't know how else to deal with it. My heart wasn't in it, because I wasn't prepared to do the things that I would normally do to support my drug habit. So I took the lazy way out and I was just driving back and forth to New York and Albany buying and selling drugs. But I also sensed that it was just a matter of time before I got busted for selling dope in Albany. It's not a wide open town and everybody around me was getting busted. I had gotten stopped on the New York Thruway a couple of times, and they never found any dope, but I knew my time was coming. And then I did finally get busted with some dope, cocaine, and reefer on the Thruway.

Obviously I was set up. They knew the car, they knew me, they knew what I was doing and where I was going. When I got to the tollbooth at exit 16 on the Thruway, I was getting ready to stick my hand out to take my toll ticket and that's when the cop cars surrounded my car. I was in the county jail for about two weeks. Joan, the nurse from the minimum-security prison, came down to bail me out. And I was fighting the case. It was in Woodbury, New York. I had to keep going back and forth to Woodbury. I still didn't have a driver's license, and the judge knew that I had to drive to Woodbury from Albany every time I had a court appearance, so all he would tell me was drive carefully. I was still intermittently using drugs at the time and fighting this case. Eventually the case was taken care of and I pled guilty to some bullshit drug charge. I got three years probation out of it. My probation was eventually transferred up to Albany, but it took months for them to do that. So in the interim, I still kept getting high. I went into the Leonard Hospital Detox Unit in Troy once during that time and detoxed from the heroin for two weeks and then they sent me to a Salvation Army center in the Albany area.

I was clean for a while, but everybody in the Salvation Army center was getting high. That's not the place to go to get your shit together. But again, I was kind of cut off from people because I really didn't have anybody that I confided in or opened up to anymore. I just didn't have the network set up that's conducive to recovery. So essentially, I was still kind of lost. And I started dipping and dabbing again with drugs. During this time, my papers came up from Woodbury and I had to start reporting to a probation officer in Albany. I left the Salvation Army joint because all I was doing was stealing. I mean, everybody was stealing and everybody was getting high. So I got a job working for a law firm as a legal administrative assistant. They were mainly immigration lawyers.

I lied on the job application, which I've done a thousand times. So I still had my habit, I'm still making trips back and forth to New York, and I'm still holding down this job. I'd get off work at 5:00 and I'd be in New York at 7:00; and be back in Albany like midnight, get up the next morning and go to work. I was selling dope from my job at the law office. I had people calling me up right there, and I'd meet them downstairs and sell them some dope.

So essentially, I was on my way back down again. I was still dipping and dabbing. I was still getting high. I had to have it. I had just gotten another apartment, which I was paying for, but the money I was making from the job wasn't enough. I was making five, six, seven times more money selling dope. During this time I had gotten stopped by the Drug Enforcement Agency in Jersey, and I walked away from that. And a friend of mine had told me that I must have nine lives the way that I live. One thing led to another and I sort of figured maybe he miscounted, and maybe I already had spent my last life. And at the same time, I was turning in dirty urine samples to my probation officer. Every time he gave me a urine test it would come up with heroin in it. And finally, I went back into Leonard Detox, this time because I had quit the job at the law firm since it wasn't enough money. I was getting disillusioned with just working and paying rent. This was all I was doing. I didn't have any other outside life. I didn't really have any friendly social contacts. Again, I was isolated.

I had gotten a speeding ticket when I had gotten back into the Albany area. A cop stopped me and they took my car. So here I am without a car and basically without an apartment, because I'm living on the highways. You know, I'm driving down to New York for a couple of hours, coming back up to Albany for a couple of hours, and then driving back down again to New York and returning to Albany. So I didn't feel the need to spend the money to pay rent on an apartment. This routine went on for a couple of months. I had a little bit of money, and I was trying to find a way to get back down to New York because my car was gone, and I didn't want the expense of taking a bus. I stopped by Lila's house, a female customer of mine who was a bull dyke, and she suggested I go back to Leonard Detox, get on welfare, and let welfare set me up with an apartment. At this particular time I had shot up all the dope that I had and I didn't have any money either. So going into detox, cleaning up for a couple of weeks, and picking up a check from welfare in order to start all over again sounded good to me. I went back to live at the detox unit again for the second time.

When I went to Leonard Detox, I had two counselors there, Guido, who was my old counselor from the first time I went through the program, and Rudy, the new head counselor. For some reason they started to make sense to me about cleaning up. And that there was a way to do it. I had explained to them the hopelessness of my situation: no place to go, no money, no family, nothing to look forward to. What am I going to do? Part of the routine of being in detox is that you attend AA meetings. This was difficult for me, because I was physically withdrawing from the heroin, plus I really wasn't in the frame of mind where I wanted to go to AA and hear all that shit that AA was talking. But if I wanted to stay in a hospital or complete the program, I had to go to the AA meetings. Also, there were little group sessions once or twice a day. So you didn't just lay up in a hospital bed. There were doctors there and while they didn't take care of all of your medical problems, they at least made you aware of any medical problems you had. The ones that they could address, they did. Rudy used to talk to me, and what he said made sense. Rudy offered me something at that point that I hadn't had in a long time: a straight-up friendship. He didn't look at me as if I had something to prove to him or that there was such a big difference between the level that he was at and the level that I was at. Rudy helped a lot, not exactly by what he said but a lot by what he didn't say.

Something different started to happen at this point, which was absent in my earlier recovery attempt at the Allen Addicts Rehabilitation Center. The basis for my therapeutic recovery—for keeping my sobriety—at ARC was more or less: stay away from drugs, talk about it once in a while, and you'll be OK. Again, this was in the early seventies. That just didn't work. When I went into the detox unit this time, I started to open up to a lot of different views. I really wasn't ready to start getting high, and by getting the chemical out of my system and clearing my head a little bit, I started to become aware of some different issues that I just wasn't aware of before. The people related to you differently in the detox unit because it's only a fourteen day detox. It's geared that way. You're not cured when you come out of there; you've detoxed yourself of the chemical, but you still need more intense follow-up. But it's a beginning, because what's happening is you have to start to get into a different mind-set. Your body is free of the chemical at this point, but recovery isn't about physically leaving the drug alone or just putting down the drug. You have to go through a mental recovery also, which is continuous. Recovery is a continuous process that you have to go through *every day of your life*. And this particular detox unit is where I became aware of these things. And I was fortunate that I ran into Rudy, a head counselor there and a recovering addict himself.

Rudy offered me something that I had been missing in my life for a long time: a friendship that was unconditional. I had just come in off the street, I was a recovering dope fiend and I was more concerned with what I didn't have. Rudy related to me on the points that I did have, and that was different. It didn't matter to him that I was a dope fiend. I didn't have to prove anything to him. And he offered himself to me with no strings, no restrictions, no nothing. And that was something new for me. Because I had been used to living in the world where nothing is real, especially not friendship. That in itself was refreshing, and I guess it started to open me up a little bit, because other things started to reach me too. But again, I wasn't cured and I still wasn't ready to be cured. I had a checkup, blood test, all types of tests. I began to eat again, which was good. And I had a few more options in there than I had when I was on the street.

When it came time for me to be released, the counselors had come to the conclusion that I should go to a rehab program as far away from Albany as possible. And at first I was adamantly against going to a rehab program, because I had been through rehab before and I didn't want to go through it again, and I couldn't see why I needed it. But then I thought, why am I in such a hurry to leave detox and return to the street when I don't really have any place to return to? So it sort of made sense for me, even in a hiding-out-sort of way; like, I'll go to rehab until I can get something together. So that was my idea.

They sent me to the St. Lawrence Alcohol Treatment Center in Ogdensburg, New York. It was an eight week program, and while I was there I attended many more AA meetings. There were counselors and also a doctor there. And this is where I really started to turn around, I guess. I had played games there for like five or six weeks. One day I went into a counselor's office and he saw I still had a lot of game in me, but he also saw that I was sincere about really wanting to recover. But I was just at the point where I didn't know how. I really did need people. And it's hard for me to reach out. It's hard for me to trust anybody. I mean, emotions are just things that I normally don't do, because they are considered weaknesses, and weaknesses are exploited on the street, and so you sort of learn to cover all of that up. You sort of hide the feelings or emotions, because they are considered weaknesses. And when you're living in a predatory society, the weak die quickly.

I was in the Ogdensburg rehab program seven or eight weeks. And that's when I really began to open up. I became acquainted with the AA twelve step self-help program. And I started to become aware of some of the issues that I really needed to deal with. And I also became aware that I needed a foundation for my recovery. I just couldn't vow to stay away from drugs and it was going to be all right. The twelve step program gave me a foundation for my recovery. I also began to believe in myself again. I actually got hungry when I was in detox after talking to Rudy. I got motivated a little bit. And when I got to the rehab program in Ogdensburg, I started to get more hungry, because I started to feel that I could focus my life again: that I could live without getting high. It was pretty important for me to really believe that. I mean, I always knew it, but I didn't really believe it.

The Ogdensburg program had group therapy sessions and individual sessions. They had a program set up for bringing you back into the mainstream of life. A crucial feature of the rehab experience was to begin to see yourself as an individual who can function normally without the use of narcotics or alcohol. And this is very hard because I didn't think that I could really live or function or find life tolerable without the use of heroin. These people began to show me that it is possible. Even though there were some times in my life that I was clean, I never really had a solid foundation, something strong to base that abstinence on. It was just willpower that I didn't get high. I was running away from it. I never really addressed the central issues.

When I got to Ogdensburg, I finally admitted that I'm a dope fiend. There were times in my life when I went into Allen's ARC place, the Bernstein Institute, and the rest of the other drug joints, but I never really wanted to stop getting high. My idea was to prove that I could get strong to a point where I could get high just on the weekends or that I could control the dope; you know, that I could clean up, control my drug habit and kick New York City in the ass. And that's bullshit — nobody does that, nobody. Everybody that I have known that has gotten strung out on dope loses. Nobody wins. But always in the back of my head, I just wanted to clean up. I had never admitted that I was a dope fiend. I always felt that I could beat the heroin addiction — that I could play with this fire without getting burned — this *tragic magic*.

I had to finally admit that my life was out of control because of my use of narcotics. *I am a dope fiend.* I like drugs. I like the way they make me feel. I am prone to use drugs to answer any problems that I experience in my life. Once recognizing this and admitting this, then I also had to admit that I need help. I need support in doing this. I couldn't do it on my own. Again, all these dynamics are contrary to my lifestyle. Asking for help, looking inside myself, reaching out; these are the things that just weren't part of my lifestyle. In fact, I did the complete opposite, which I guess tells you why my life has been fucked up for so long.

SEEING THAT I WAS SOMEWHAT MOTIVATED, the counselors at Ogdensburg suggested I go to a halfway house in Canton,

New York. They knew that I needed more support than they could give me. Again, detox is only set up to detoxify you chemically from whatever it is that you're abusing. Rehab is only designed to take you so far. A halfway house is designed, I guess, to provide a more or less final step before you come back out. I was sort of against that idea, too, but again I didn't have any other place to go, so in 1989 I went to Canton.

The halfway house, I suppose, is like halfway between your addiction and the outside world again. It's designed to reacquaint you with society. And I'm grateful that I was fortunate enough to come to this particular halfway house. They have a way of dealing with people that I think is essential towards anyone's recovery. They were kind, they were understanding, they were stern, and they were very, very helpful, especially Ray Hernandez, a counselor there. Ray is a recovering alcoholic and he has a way with people that's just simply magic. He doesn't pity you but he relates to you in such a way where you begin to feel a little self-esteem. When he points out things that you do wrong, he doesn't do it in a way that you feel guilty, or that you want to hide from. I mean, he does it in such a way where it's okay to do this, and it's okay to feel that at that time, but you need to improve on that. And he's willing to work with you and he's willing to hang right in there. And this point in your life is very delicate, especially when it comes to relating to people again. Because normally dope fiends don't deal with people or personal problems or situations—we just get high. And a lot of recovering addicts find it very difficult to deal with people. Ray has a way of letting you know that you're not alone. And I guess for me at that point, like a lot of other people, it's essential that you know that you're not alone.

At the halfway house we learned to discuss important issues like self-esteem, value clarification, denial, stress, relapse, relationships, communication, human sexuality. And I felt funny going through a human sexuality class because I thought I was very secure in my manhood, and I found out that my sexual values were just as screwed up as everybody else's. And emotions—we used to have a feelings group every Monday for an hour and a half. And I didn't really look forward to these sessions, because they get deep. But this is what helps: being able to get in touch with your emotions again, being able to identify what you feel. You have to know these things in order to know what to deal with and how to deal with it. But these are delicate areas and most recovering people are emotional misfits. They haven't touched their emotions; they haven't dealt with them. And I was shielding my emotions with my use of heroin.

I stayed in the halfway house for about seven months. But Ray—and Rudy, too—are still part of my support network. And I still stay in contact with both of them. These are two people that I have developed a trust and respect for, and I listen to. These people are vital to my survival at this point, because instead of stuffing an issue, and not dealing with it, and having it come out in a negative way, or having me run back to using dope again, if there's something bothering me, I'll bring it out. And I'm not close to a lot of people. But because I'm coming through recovery and coming through rehab and dealing with Ray, I know that I need to address whatever it is that's bothering me.

It has been six months since I left the halfway house. Since then I've made plans to enroll in Mater Dei College, a small private Catholic two-year school near Ogdensburg. I've also volunteered to work inside St. Lawrence County Jail, where I facilitate AA meetings. I'm involved in the Ogdensburg Correctional Facility on Thursday evenings where I've facilitated both AA and NA meetings. I've given lectures at St. Lawrence University. I've been fortunate through that opportunity to get invitations to lecture out of the state. I'm a percussionist and this spring semester I've been doing the percussion for the dance classes at Potsdam State College.

My involvement in NA in the prison is important, because it keeps my experiences green to me. It brings them right in front. In other words, I can't forget who and what I am: a recovering heroin addict. And if I get away from the situation, I'll tend to forget that. And once I tend to forget that, that's bringing me right back on the road to using drugs again. Because then I'll think that I'm strong enough. But by being able to relate to some of the prison population, it keeps it real green for me, because every time I walk in that prison I remember. I am a dope fiend. The minute that I forget that I'm a dope fiend, I'm that much closer to my next shot of dope.

I KNOW WHERE I WANT TO GO. I also realize that now I have a foundation for my recovery. Should I have problems, whether it's directly related to drugs or not, I've built up a network of people that I can go to. And I've learned to reach out and I've learned to trust. I'm not a religious person but I've also made spiritual progress. I stay in touch with these people and places and things, because this is what's helping me to readjust. And this is what's helping me in my recovery.

I miss not being able to spend more time with my daughter Kimberly, who's fifteen years old now. But I can't do this recovery just for her. Kimberly can't help me recover. I'm the only one that can do this for me. It's kind of selfish, but I look at it this way: how much can I do for her if I'm still out there in the street? There have been times when I've been in prison or I have been around Kimberly and we've dealt with that. I talk to Kimberly now. We write and talk on the phone. She's living in the Bronx now with her mother and goes to a private day school in the Bronx. In September she's going to a boarding school in Boston on a scholarship. She's always been in private schools. Kimberly is academically gifted, and we tried her in public school for about a year, but she surpassed that. I've contributed only a little to financing her private school education. I feel kind of bad about that, but I'm putting myself in an eventual position where I can go back and address that. In the meantime, Kimberly keeps the doors open for communication. She says she understands, and she's willing to go along with that until I can get to a better position. I hope that's how she feels. When she was younger and I was there, I took care of her, and she knows that. So I'm guessing that she knows that there's something not right, which is why I'm not able to contribute that way now. But it's not because I don't want to.

I don't know where my son Jason is. I had contact with him until he was about ten years old. Lucille and I had separated and divorced long before that, but I still was in touch with Jason because I knew where Lucille lived. In later years

I lost contact with where she moved, and it was hard for me to keep in contact with my son. I tried to look up Lucille from the old neighborhood and old friends, her mother and what have you, but everybody has moved. The last time I saw Jason was about two years before I went to prison. He was maybe between eight and ten years old. We really used to be attached, real, real close. I feel kind of shitty because I don't feel good about being a father, and I wonder what he's doing. And I wonder what influence I could have as far as doing something positive in his life or even doing something for him.

Right now my goal is to eventually go back into the criminal justice field. I understand that I need a college credential to do that. School is my immediate goal. I'm committing myself to the North Country right now, because this is where I've made my new life, my new surroundings. I've committed myself long enough to go to school. After that, I'm going to have to reevaluate where I'm going in terms of job and additional schooling. I would eventually like to go back into the prisons and be sort of a go-in-between for the inmates and administration, and the inmates and the outside. I think someone should make them aware that there's a transition process that they have to go through. And being in prison, you don't get much support or much motivation towards rehabilitation. Prisons don't rehabilitate; they warehouse. And having come through that system myself, I think it's a waste of life to have someone go into prison, come back out, do another crime, and then go back in. I would like to break that cycle. The only people that I met that were an influence on me in prison were negative influences.

There is, of course, a danger that I'll get burned out or ground up by the prison bureaucracy, but knowing that possibility—and keeping the network I have now and am going to set up in the future—I hope to guard against that type of situation. I know that if I manage to get caught up in the same system and turn bureaucratic, I would lose my effectiveness. And I know in my heart that if I did get into that rut, that's not me, and that something must have happened to change me. I think I can do what I want to do and be effective just the way I am. I understand that the rules of the game are going to change, but that's why I'm going to school. I want to be qualified to go back in there and play those bullshit games and still be effective and still make a difference. Because I don't think the solution to the problem is to just lock them up. What are you going to do with them when they get out?

As a recovering drug addict looking at my life in retrospect, it's difficult to try and make some sense out of why I drifted into a life of drug addiction and remained in much of that lifestyle off and on for almost thirty years. At the time that it was happening, I didn't have any clue or idea. But looking back, I think there were a lot of gaps, a lot of holes in my life. I'm an only child. I didn't know my father. I lived with my mother and in the beginning she lived with her mother, so it was a house with two women. I don't know, maybe I had an identity problem then, too. Whenever I went to school and came home, I always came home to two women. I really didn't have a male model at home to guide me. I was never taught at home what a man is and what a man does, what a man's role is.

When my grandfather first came here from Cuba, he got into numbers. He had been running numbers for about forty or fifty years. He wasn't around when I was young on a regular basis. But the times when I was around him, I did get some feeling of being part of a family unit, and he always accepted me as being his grandson. And that always made me feel good. And every time I knew I was going to see him, I identified with the Latin part of my family, and I always felt kind of weird about that.

I was born and raised in the South Bronx, and then my mother and grandmother moved down to St. Nicholas projects in the middle of black Harlem. I think I was about seven or eight and I went to elementary school there, and started junior high school, and then we moved back up to the Bronx. But there were gaps. There were a lot of gaps. And I always felt the need for something else. I always thought that something was missing—in my life, my family. Part of that energy I channeled into academics, but I always had a problem with the social part. Even hanging out with the guys I wondered, "Who am I? What am I supposed to be? Who do I really pattern myself after?" Most of my dreams and aspirations were someone else's, one of my running partners or one of my friends; I assumed that what he wanted is what I wanted. Even being in the gangs and everything—I did it because this is what my friends wanted to do. I didn't really know what I wanted to do.

I don't think my mother was ready for the life that we were leading in Harlem either. She knew some of the people there, but she wasn't really a Harlem person. Although she wasn't religious or anything, she didn't drink and she didn't get high. My mother had a very strong work ethic and she used to work every day. When I was in the fifth or sixth grade in elementary school, I could do what I wanted each day when I got out of school since I had the key to my apartment. My grandmother was still living there, but she used to work, too, and wasn't home in the afternoons. In the beginning I would go home because this is what the rules were. So I had time to get into studies and read and practice my violin and all the other stuff that they were teaching me to do in school, because I didn't have those diversions, I guess, that other kids had. When I left school, I went straight home. I didn't hang out in the park, or I wasn't running with a gang of guys at that time. I was more or less independent.

But eventually, I started developing a different pattern. I would go out after school, because I didn't feel like staying home alone anymore. When I was maybe ten, eleven, twelve years old, I didn't really have anybody close that I could talk to about things. There was no man in my life—no father or male role model that I was close to. Everything I learned, I learned in the street from everybody else. I never let them know that they were teaching me, but I would ask questions or I would observe, and I would see things and then I would make my own decisions. But I'd never really had anybody who told me what the rule was or what the deal was. I found out on my own. Even when it came to women, I had an older woman teach me how to please and satisfy a younger woman. There were very few times that I went to my mother and asked for knowledge or guidance or anything. By the time I did start to ask my mother a few things, her answers were kind of naive, so I sort of backed away from confiding in her. My mother had a lot of friends, but she wasn't street smart. She loved me, and I know that, and she did the best that she could for me. It's just that I never clicked with her ideas.

There were always two parts of me. The academic, bright, mannerly young boy, which is who I was at home. I had manners. I said "Yes, please." I respected my elders in the house. In the street it was a different thing. I sort of had to take off my white shirt or go out on the street and put some dirt on it, you know, in order to fit in with the young people my age that were living in the projects and going to school and doing other things. And I got involved in drugs because this is what everybody else was doing during this particular period.

Again, looking back at it, I think I've always had an identity problem. And I wanted to have a family and I wanted to be able to identify with people or groups. I had been alone so much in my life that when I started to get a little older, I didn't want to be alone anymore. In order for me not to be alone, I had to be a member of a group or gang. My heart really wasn't in it, but I guess I did it to fill that loneliness gap. I even feel alone now, so I guess it's just been with me for a long time. And the gang was a kind of substitute family, because in the gang I had a father, a mother, brothers. I had somebody to look out for. I had somebody to look out for me. I did a lot of dirty negative shit in my life, and most of it was because I didn't want to feel alone.

By the time I got to heroin, I had done a lot of other drugs. And just like everything else I did in my life, I could take them or leave them. When I got to heroin, I liked it. I really liked it. Heroin made me feel like I fit in, and all I needed was the heroin. I didn't need people, I didn't need places, and I didn't need things. All I needed was the heroin.

11

MUSIC, DRUMS, AND DRUGS

I've always had this cultural identity problem. Nobody ever told me who I was and what I was. And it was through music that I began to find out these things about myself. Music is where I really discovered my Latin, my Cuban, my Afro-Cuban roots. Even when I was young, I had always been attracted to drums and percussion. When I was young growing up in Harlem, my first musical exposure was to the Motown sound—the rhythm and blues soul singers and music like that, and I liked it. But I hadn't been exposed to Latin music yet. When I moved to the Bronx and I became exposed to Latin music, I immediately took to Latin music. I knew musically and culturally that's where my musical tastes lay. I didn't know it at the time, but my grandfather was also a percussionist in Cuba. I didn't find that out until the year before he died. But I always had this feeling about music. I've always managed to live through music, even with the rhythm and blues and rock and roll. I could always listen to a tune and relate that to part of my life; the good times and the bad times, you know, I relate to that musically.

When I got to the Bronx I really got into my own heritage. I began to get to know Latin musicians, mostly drummers. I was always interested in them. Even when I went to a music

185

store, I always knew who I wanted to listen to and what I
wanted to hear. And I began to go to all the Latin dances.
By the time I wanted to start playing drums in my early
thirties, I'd already had an accident with my hand, where
I cut my nerves and tendons and I couldn't use my fingers
for a while. So I figured that would eliminate me from playing the drums, which turned out to be wrong. Through the
Latin music I began to learn more about myself, my culture, and my heritage, and that kept me around other Latin
people.

I used to hang out with guys that played in the band, and
at times even when they weren't playing in the band. One of
the guys, Mike Rivera, who's teaching percussion in Califor-
nia right now, was an excellent conga player. And I was hanging out with the singer, Noel, and this trombone player, Pablo
Conte. And they introduced me to Mikey. Mike and I sort of
took to each other and became friends. Since I was always
at the dances and always picking up the little hand instruments and stuff, Mikey asked me one day, "Why don't you
learn how to play the drums?" And I showed him my hands.
Mike said, "Man, that's nothing, I'll teach you." So he gave me
two sticks and a drum pad and some exercises. And I went
home and I listened to what he told me. Eventually Mikey
and I started hanging out. At the time, he was playing with
some of the bands in New York, but he was also the drummer for the Puerto Rican Dance Theater in New York.

Through Mike I learned a different understanding of
what drumming and percussion was all about. Mikey taught
me technique, he taught me style, and he taught me discipline on the drums. I used to respect his drum playing
because Mikey never had calluses on his hands. If a drummer had calluses on his fingers, you knew that he was a
heavy drummer. Mikey had developed a style and technique
so he didn't have to do that. You know, there was a different
way to go about drumming. There was a way to commune
with the skin and the gods without tearing up your hands.
And Mikey opened my eyes up to this. I was kind of scared
in the beginning because I knew a lot of other guys were
drummers and drummers are a dime a dozen in New York.
But what I didn't know was the discipline and everything else

that makes the difference between a drummer and a disciplined drummer. And Mikey showed me that.

Pretty soon I began to play with some of the bands in New York. At this time I had met Tavi Lopez and Danny Travino, and Danny became interested in me as a drummer. I met Danny when I was selling a lot of cocaine and doing a lot of reefer. Danny didn't have a lot of discipline, and he always wanted to play things or do things his own way, but he was a dynamite drummer. So Danny began teaching me. I am fortunate because I have learned from a drummer; I have never paid for a drumming lesson and I've never had a formal drumming lesson.

When I was in my twenties I briefly attended Johnny Colon's music school because I had decided that there was more that I wanted to learn. Mikey could only have so much time to teach me. But it was Mikey who really opened me up to so much. He used to play trap drums and also American drums. When he would play in a combo in some of these French restaurants downtown, he would take me with him. Mikey used to take me to a lot of the performances that he did. We had a good friendship as well as an apprenticeship. Mikey was into the Santería religion—spiritualism—as was his family. And they accepted me, which was strange because I'm just now starting to come into my spiritual cultural roots. But there were things that I always knew about drumming. I just knew it. And Mikey sort of opened the door a little bit more about it—about the spiritual connection anyway. Mikey also told me in the beginning not to disrespect the spirits and get high when I played because they'll get upset. I took that to heart. I've never played high off of anything. Because I would be disrespecting the spirits and I was kind of scared of that.

COCAINE, HEROIN, AND POT were big parts of the musical scene. You've got black musicians right now whose lives are still messed up because of the use of heroin. I've played with dope fiends and coke heads. They couldn't play unless they got high. I found it quite the opposite for myself. It used to bother me a little bit because when we did rehearsals they would be getting high and I couldn't. It was just a part of my life where I knew that I couldn't get involved with drugs. But after rehearsal I went and got fucked up. At the time I was mainly into burglarizing and robbing places to support my habit. But during the time that I was performing, I didn't touch anything.

Some individuals claim to have their musical abilities enhanced by the use of drugs. My musical skills are diluted by the use of any type of drugs. But there are guys that I know that get high—they get spaced out—and then they go off into all types of creative things. I can play with a guy and I wouldn't know automatically if he was high or not. This again shows you part of the allure and the destructive use of what these drugs can do. These guys got to the point where they felt that they could not perform unless they were high. And I know guys that are excellent musicians. I mean, they have God-given skills. They don't need drugs to enhance what they can do. And, in fact, they don't perform up to par. I've done gigs with guys that were fine trumpet players and the first set sounded like shit. They went and got high and sounded great the rest of the night. I feel it's definitely psychological. Like when I was getting high off all of these other drugs outside of the musical context, I felt more creative and wild and uninhibited. But when it came to my music, I did not want to disrespect the spirits and bring a bad spirit down to do his shit on me. So I was afraid of that. There were times when I would go home and I'd smoke a joint, or I'd be high and I'd start to work out on my drums, and I'd fuck that up, so I'd leave it alone. I walked away from that.

When I was high off a reef of pot, I would hear things and I would feel things and I would trip out off the music. But I also found that when I listen to music sober I can listen to a record one hundred times and that next time hear something that I never heard before. So I don't think my sensibility to music is due to the drugs. But that's my personal opinion. I know people that it doesn't matter if they're high or not. They play.

I love playing Latin timbales, Latin conga drums, African drums, especially the djimbe. I love the sound of those drums. Later on in life when I moved to Albany, I got involved with an African dance group. Up until that time all my drumming had been Latin percussion, and I loved it. I got hip that there's not just Puerto Rican Latin music, but there are those sounds from all the different Latin countries; and there are different ways to play their Spanish music. Yet somehow, I always felt like I was missing something. Again, this is nothing anybody told me; this is just something that I felt, something that I knew.

When I got to Albany, I got involved with a Latin cultural folklorico group. So the Latin music that we played was mostly drum—raw drum. And most of the Latin musicians didn't really want to give due respect to the roots of what they were playing. It's all African in root. There was something missing in me and the spirits made me reach out. And one day I saw a performance by an African dance group in Albany, and after that performance I went to the director of the dance group and asked him if they would be willing to teach me Afro drumming since I was a Latin drummer. And that's when I became involved in the Burundi African Dance Troupe. And I knew I had found my roots then. I love playing Afro and I played with Burundi for five years. At the time, I was still selling dope, going back and forth between Albany and New York. But I never got high when I did a performance. And I never got high at rehearsal. It was always long before and immediately after, but I never shot dope when I played.

Burundi was probably the longest stretch I played with one particular musical group, because in New York it's not so much playing with just one group since you get to be more like a replaceable part. You play with one group tonight, or you might play with three different groups in the same night. I started out with one group of guys and they eventually started going to different bands. Playing with one group and keeping it very cohesive is just a difficult thing to do.

Because musicians in New York are a dime a dozen, most of the musicians that I knew and played with had full-time jobs. It's very difficult to make it just on your instrument alone, and I never thought that I could make it a career. There are musicians that do that and I guess they have an extra added something. The two people that are most influential in my life as far as drumming is concerned are Tavi Lopez and Danny Travino. Tavi has a full-time factory job. And I mean Tavi is good. He plays with the top Latin bands today on weekends but the money is not that great. I also had this fear because of my hands. If something should happen to my hands and I can't play, I can't get paid. But if I could have it my way, music would be my vocation and every other minute of my life would be filled with dedication to my music. At this point I just can't get into music primarily as a source of income, but music—Afro, Cuban percussion—will always be a part of my life.

Music in prison is one of the things that saved my sanity. At every institution that I went to, I played in the prison band, from Bronx County Jail to Rikers Island. The only place I didn't play was Downstate because I wasn't there long enough. When I got to Sing Sing I played and when I got to the upstate joints I played. In every place I went I was fortunate that there was already either a banged up drum or a drum that needed a head or something. My music was my escape. At Rikers Island, we used to lock out twice a day for band practice because we had a CO named Hemilly, who was in charge of the music program, and he was serious about his music. At Rikers, I got to know some of the Marielitos, the boat people from Cuba. A lot of them were serious musicians, and I used to drum with them in the band. Because I was also Cuban, I got to know a lot of them and heard a lot of their stories. Castro emptied out all the prisons and all the mental institutions in Cuba. He told them, "If you want to leave, get the hell out—go to America." Consequently, a lot of the Marielitos that came across were criminals. Eventually, a number of them filtered up to New York City, and it was like a new world. Many of these guys were committing heavy crimes. I met some that were getting arrested and indicted for multiple homicide. There were a couple of guys in Rikers Island from the city that were fighting murder charges and getting like fifteen to life, twenty-five to life, fifty to life. And here come these guys from Cuba, and they've got five or six or seven dead bodies. Whether drugs were involved or not, they just came to New York and were killing people. Not arguing, just killing people.

I learned a lot from the inmates at Rikers Island. We used to lock out in the morning and once in the afternoon, and we'd go to the auditorium for rehearsal. And we would do in-house shows for the inmates. One of the top Latin violinists, Alfredo De La Fe, was on Rikers Island. He got busted for possession of a lot of cocaine and he used to do shows in the summertime. Music was the only thing that saved me during my whole time there, because if I hadn't been able to play, I think things would have been different. But I had gotten my frustrations off by playing. I also got special privileges by being in the band, especially with Hemilly. Since Rikers Island is in New York City, we used to get to see a lot of Broadway shows. They would come over and do benefit shows for the inmates. And because we were part of that musical thing, Hemilly would get the band members seats right in front and we got to meet a lot of the people that did these shows.

I HAVE BEEN TOLD — and I know — that if I could apply the same discipline and respect that I have for my music to the rest of my life, it would be a lot more disciplined and things would be a lot more organized. When it comes to my music, I respect my drums, I respect my music. I have a spiritual connection that just is there. I don't question it and I let it guide me. If I could apply that same belief, faith, and everything else into what I do in my outside life, my life would be a little more coherent. When I'm with my music and when I'm with my drums, there is no heroin. There's no room for drugs. There's no getting high. I have the ultimate respect for my instruments. And because of the connection with the spirits and everything else, there's no danger of my instruments opening a door for me back to drugs, because my instruments were never connected to my drug habit. For me music and dope are two different worlds. If I stay in my musical world, there's no need for me to use drugs. I get high off my drums. I get high listening to music. Playing music is tantamount to having an orgasm with a female. That's how strong it is for me.

My music keeps me sane, you know. Reaching for my percussion roots keeps me sane. It also educates me. Because the more I get into my music, the more I learn about my culture. And the more I learn about my culture, the more I learn about me. So there's a definite connection there. And I will never give that up. And I will always play. Always. When I perform, I don't perform for money. Money is not what motivates me to play. Just like when I worked in the prison: I did that on a voluntary basis because I feel a need to give back some of the things that were given to me. And my music is the same way. I play for the enjoyment of the people. But I will sit here and play for myself, which I do a lot, because I need it for my own self-edification. Money, gifts, and things like that do not motivate me to play. As a matter of fact, it dilutes my performance, and that has happened to me a couple of times. I'm not that type of musician. I know musicians who can perform for the money and then turn right off. I can't do that. I have to be motivated, stimulated to play, which is why I loved performing with the Burundi African Dance Troupe. The relationship between me and the other drummers and dancers was just something that was nonmaterial.

I would love to get deeply involved again with an African percussion group. I'd like to play in a Latin band, but I would also like to get involved in an African dance troupe. There are still a lot of things that I've got to learn, and the rhythms stimulate me since drums are an integral part of African society. The whole lifestyle, the whole culture, the whole civilization. And drumming is a language itself. And one of my wishes is to go to Africa sometime in the future and just sit down in the village; and with the permission of the elders and the master drummers, just watch and listen. I get taken away when I get into my drumming. I don't know, it takes me into a different world, a different time.

If I'm able to go back into prison to work with inmates, I hope my use of music may make it easier to communicate or develop rapport. Whether it's Afro, Latin, or whatever, music is the message. Music sometimes gets through to people when words don't. You don't have to speak Spanish to like Spanish music. You don't have to speak Swahili in order to understand or feel what an African rhythm can do for you. I think percussion reaches a primal chord in everyone. Even people that don't know when it's there respond to percussion.

And I think that having that available as another avenue, as another form of communication, is a plus. At this point, I don't see it being of major use, but it would be nice to have it as an extra added dimension to help me communicate. But, again, it's not just musical tones and rhythms; there's an education involved in what I do. Different rhythms come from different places. And they all have a story. I think I'm finding more out about myself as far as playing the types of instruments I like to play. They're all natural. I mean conga drums are skin on skin, your hands on top of the skin. They're made of wood. All of the original instruments were made of wood. The flute, the guitar, the drums. They're all natural instruments which you can find in natural surroundings.

I think another door of knowledge has opened, and my pursuit of music, or my percussion at this point, is only going to enhance me and enlighten me. I'm learning facts now that I never knew. And instead of intellectually taking them apart, it's simpler to accept them as being natural. I mean, there's no way to dispute that. I'm coming more into myself and finding out what I'm about and feeling comfortable with what I find out. I don't have to try to explain a bunch of things intellectually. I can explain it very simply. And I believe what I'm hearing. And it's sort of like my gut feeling or my inner sense is guiding me in which direction to go. That's easier for me to take. I don't go in any direction now that's too complicated. I feel if it's not the way for me to go, I leave it alone. And I'm guided, I guess, in my musical or my percussion journey. And there's a spiritual connection which I'm just starting to really get into. And so far it hasn't been negative; it has only helped me. It has broadened me as an individual, and I think the more I come to it, the more I can relate to someone else. Or maybe I can make their journey a little shorter. I'm not saying that mine is the right way or the only way, it's just a way. And it's a way that if I'm comfortable with I can explain it to someone else. If it works for me, it's a possibility that it might work for someone else. Or through that they might find the door that they're looking for. Maybe this is like a common ground, or a point of less confusion for them to see which way that they want to go.

POSTSCRIPT

On February 8, 1991, while enrolled in college, Ron Santiago was stopped by a state trooper for speeding in Jefferson County, N.Y. A police computer check revealed that Ron was operating a car without a valid license and had walked away from fifteen traffic tickets and motor vehicle violations accumulated over the years amounting to more than $1,200 in unpaid fines. An irate local judge fined Ron $375 and sentenced him to four days in the county jail in Watertown.

On the same day in February, a *Watertown Daily Times* newspaper article listed Ron as one of a handful of students who made the President's List for having received a perfect 4.0 grade point average during the preceding academic semester at Mater Dei College. In May, 1991, Ron Santiago successfully completed his first year of college.

— SLH

RON'S PRISON POEMS

What Am I Doing Here?

Had the world by the ass
Had lots of cash
 Had not a care or a fear,
Went many places
Met many new faces
 What am I doing here?

I drove in nice cars
To all the hip bars
 Had fun both far and near,
Had many a whirl
with plenty of girls
 What am I doing here?

I thought I was fly
And stayed pretty high
 My life flowed in high gear,
Things were just grand
I even played in a band
 What am I doing here?

197

Now, I'm not really bad
Though I'm often a cad
    Most times I think I'm pretty fair,
A dummy I'm not
And good sense I've got
    What am I doing here?

I was college educated
Even career dedicated
    Had the things men hold most dear,
With a girl child so sweet
And the world at my feet
    What am I doing here?

Well, I committed a crime
And am now doing time
    But one thing is still unclear
If I had all of this
And was so close to bliss
    What the FUCK am I doing here???

—Ron Santiago
  82 A 0932

The Beast

When you're young it seems
Life is made up of dreams
    And a lot of stories, you are told,
But then comes your turn
To disturbingly learn
    That all that glitters is not gold.

Things are equal it's said
You can make plenty of "bread"
    Anything can be arranged,
Then comes the panic
If you're Black or Hispanic
    When you learn the rules have changed.

198

So what do you do
If you can't be true
    To yourself, or anyone else?
You use your smarts
Conceal your inner parts
    And learn how to handle yourself.

School loses its attraction
Working's no satisfaction
    Now enter the world of the insane,
Always on the run
SURVIVAL becomes
The real name of the game.

The jungle creed
Says the strong must feed
    On any prey at hand,
I was branded a beast
And sat at the feast
    Before I was a man.

I took my place at the table
And did whatever I was able
    Turned into a thing most rotten,
I put on my mask
And joined the cast
    Of the "Theatre of the Forgotten."

Hardship and grief and strife
They all become a way of life
    And many things you're not able to see,
Life could be bright and gay
It doesn't have to be this way
    You yourself hold the key.

But some are pre-ordained
To be forever contained
    No escape possible in the least,
And to that selection
There is no protection
    From the belly of the Beast!

—Ron Santiago
  82 A 0932